Summer's Memory

Summer's Memory

The Autumn Sequel

For all too soon -
The Seasons of a Music Teacher

Richard E. Taesch

Richard E. Taesch

Copyright © 2023 by Richard E. Taesch

All rights reserved. No part of this book may be reproduced in any manner whatsoever without written permission except in the case of brief quotations embodied in critical articles and reviews.

First Printing, 2023

to
a little dog named "Kindness,"
and the little girl who loved her

CONTENTS

EARLY AUTUMN

I | Transitions — 2

II | What can it all mean? — 10

III | So you want to be a music teacher! — 20

IV | Summer memories — 33

V | Reflections — 42

VI | What if... — 51

VII | Reflections from the bandstands — 61

VIII | As you believe — 67

IX | Highlights — 76

X | The cynics — 82

XI | Careers — 86

XII | Strangers — 93

CONTENTS

xiii ❙ Ports in the storms 2021   99

xiv ❙ Dreams   105

xv ❙ Gratitude, Ignorance, & Philosophy   110

xvi ❙ Routes of passage   118

xvii ❙ Karma   125

MID AUTUMN

xviii ❙ Millennium meanderings   136

xix ❙ How to fail at business and still celebrate life   145

xx ❙ Remembrances nearly forgotten   151

xxi ❙ Little joys   159

xxii ❙ My world in autumn   164

xxiii ❙ Autumn's parting thoughts   174

xxiv ❙ The closing story of one man's mission   182

ACKNOWLEDGMENTS   195

AN INTRODUCTION TO AUTUMN

Why authors write their own stories

The purpose and motivation for publishing one's own story has been pondered by many writers over time. Perhaps in the beginning, one may simply hope that his or her stories are so unique and special that consumers will stand in line to read them. Others may feel an inflated self-image and consider their story as a kind of gift to humanity, while secretly coveting a best seller list for monetary aspirations.

However, whether an author was a famed dignitary, popular celebrity, past president or monarch, I truly believe that - deep inside - we all feel a hidden connection and alignment to our fellow humans. We simply hold a desire to share with them. Fundamentally, we all have unique yet similar stories with personal variants. Few are able to take the time out to write about them, or have the desire to explore a learning curve required of a professional in any field. It has been said by one legendary educator that writing cannot be taught, only helped.

To me, when a writer takes on such a calling, professional or amateur, he or she soon becomes immersed in the experience as opposed to the motivation. One proceeds on behalf of all of us as though one in spirit. Meaning that, the human predicament pertains to everyone collectively. Therefore, *Summer's Memory* is Richard's passion to continue extending *For all too soon* to his readers. It is his way to share experiences having matured, aged, and collected a bit of "tude" (attitude) along the way. Welcome to autumn, as with some luck, may we all arrive there sooner or later. As said in winter through summer, I have written about then, while remaining ever aware that this is now.

AN INTRODUCTION TO AUTUMN

For clarification sake, some reprints have been included here. All have a new purpose and perhaps a new life in the time frames as we enter the last season. And as any book by the same author, new readers are always precious. To share old stories in new context is then again *new* to the author and to past readers.

And for the new and past reader, may I briefly define the differences between *Short Stories, Vignettes,* and *Outtakes* as appear in the structural strategy of this work. Vignettes and Outtakes are simply my situational and spontaneous recollections or accountings. Whereas, Short Stories are thought of as microcosmic novels within themselves. They often contain non-fiction players with fictional names. However, they represent real life and real stories.

And so, if Richard can leave this world one day feeling that he has done his best to contribute some things to ponder in his little stories, then maybe, just maybe there might be a glimmer of hope for others to turn the tides into a new millennium of healing and wisdom.

THE SEASONS*
by Richard Taesch

Winter

I am often dark and cold – I am here to remind you of your own self, but I am also here to give you the gift of spring ...

Spring

I am peace – I am your new life – spend time with me in the green quiet places, **for all too soon,** *I will be gone ...*

Summer

I am quiet – noisy – hot – cool – a time for different things – a time to remember the coolness of winter, and to anticipate the new beginning ...

AN INTRODUCTION TO AUTUMN

Fall / Autumn

I am mature, stately, and proud – my beauty can only be seen by those who walk with me in solitude – I am summer's memory ...

*Quoted by permission from: *Introduction to the Piano for the Blind Student,* Book 1, Repertoire, by Richard Taesch (2000) – Southern California Conservatory of Music – Braille Music Division [Published by Dancing Dots, www.dancingdots.com]

Autumn on 34th Street

EARLY AUTUMN

Transitions

Autumn

*I am mature, stately, and proud – my beauty can only be seen by those who walk with me in solitude – I am **summer's memory** ... The Seasons* - R. Taesch

For all too soon, Richard began to sense that his life-long career in music was beginning to tremble at its footings. The *troubled years* resulting from conflicts during the latter years of Southern California Conservatory of Music's (SCCM) *Braille Music Division,* along with economic woes for non-profits during 2008, saw the final curtain begin to slowly descend. But alas, his musical life had also been bountifully rich with wonderful students who had achieved many exciting things. Here's to them and to my colleagues who helped build a legacy that will hopefully live on through time!

But nonetheless, even the longest of careers in education can be affected by age, fatigue, and the usual paradigm shifts of time and trends. For example, communication technology that introduced Big Brother into private music lessons. His dreaded "Notification" aloud, or ring tones from the twilight zone emanating from a student's I-phone prompted me to silently yearn for retirement on more than one occasion. Trying to conduct music study with such interruptions was not unlike a siren demanding that you pull over to allow an emergency vehicle to pass - the call usually won. A parent auditing his or her child's lesson while merrily chatting away on a device was not unlike trying to teach a lesson in an international airport waiting area. Yikes!

Although such experiences may seem somewhat comedic and playfully accounted, my own retirement was clearly not my preference. I loved them all, even though I often viewed my millennium-era students' phones as a kennel of barking dogs in the same room. A cacophony it was, no matter. Yet rest assured that Richard always left for home at the end of the day, happy, and loving his job.

In the introduction, I stated that this *fall* sequel to my winter through summer remembrance would include some outcomes resulting from beyond that time in the form of short stories and vignettes. Speaking of technology and paradigms, the first one should fit well into this chapter about transition.

This first collection will then venture somewhat beyond *summer* stories as written in *For all too soon*. More will come later in a similar form. The chronology of events is mostly random, although grouped together within chapter titles. Some consist of a kind of fallout of effects with a hint of lingering impressions and revelations stemming from the *troubled years*.

The reprinted article that follows appeared in our *Music Education Network for The Visually Impaired* (MENVI) newsletter in 2004, Issue 17. It is a tongue-in-cheek effort to advocate for music braille literacy in a time when such a thing was considered by many as *far too complex* to be of much use. Today, only fifteen years later, music reading in braille is an accepted skill required of blind college entrants into most music departments.

RICHARD E. TAESCH

SHORT STORIES - Points & Views #1

INCREDIBLE "NEW" TECHNOLOGY FOR THE BLIND!
[Edited Reprint - with permission]

It has come to our attention that a new access technology for visually impaired individuals has been discovered. We have all heard of an early device that - when placed upon one's head - enabled a blind person to actually see print. It was capable of transmitting a print image directly to the brain of a blind individual.

Upon *seeing* print music, a blind MENVI specialist once commented: "How do you guys read that stuff?" Well, considering the visual art and graphic nature of print music, one might understand why digital technology has become so popular. (A note of trivia: Morse and International [telegraphic] code is radio's oldest form of digital communication.)

The technology we are speaking of is a medium capable of bypassing the eye and allowing a blind person not only to see the printed and spoken word directly in the brain, but even to hear music by touch! In its most basic form, this medium requires no expensive and complex equipment - no electricity, no batteries! In fact, it is available to everyone anywhere who desires independence.

Imagine! A blind user can actually place his or her finger upon this device and instantly actualize any print text or music notation medium that is available to the sighted. This "new" technology is called *Braille*.

Like the International or Morse code, braille is truly a ... *direct human digital communications mode* ...* Incredible technology, indeed!

**American Radio Relay League (ARRL) Southwestern Division Newsletter*, January, 2004.

The Dawning of a star

The good years in my *summer* brought many special things into our lives at SCCM, not the least of which was little Rebecca Dawning at age 4.5. Well, she is no longer "little," as now in her mid-twenties (See *For all too soon* - Page 256). Good fortune always seemed to follow her as to opportunities: scholarship funding, donated instruments, friends, gifted talents, and a loving family.

She began performing professionally very early and gaining notice by some well-known celebrities. Club dates, CD recordings, Internet, etc., eventually led to a full-length documentary movie about her life from a blind child to becoming a gifted and extremely competent musician/composer who plays many instruments.

Though rarely mentioned in promotions and event announcements, her ability to read music in braille is perhaps her most stunning accomplishment! As a child, she often towered above her sighted peers in sight reading, and took the highest honors at early and secondary orchestra festivals. Clearly, Rebecca rendered those who made such skills possible for her, very, very proud!

Sadly, some publicity announcements sometimes give educator credits inaccurately. At times, they seem to play down braille music reading skills of a blind, educated, and literate musician. For Rebecca, it was often the image of an anomaly who gallantly overcame her disability. Nothing could be further from the truth. Rebecca was simply gifted from birth, had the best instruction possible, and worked diligently to succeed!

During production and publicity about the documentary, my colleague and I were expected to appear in the movie. We both found ways to avoid that happening; few knew any reason why we would pass up such an opportunity. At this point, it seems appropriate to reveal - for the first time - at least my own reason for remaining *behind the curtain*, so to speak.

Our VI program at the conservatory consisted of many very deserving and musically talented blind youngsters. Rebecca always seemed to gather the most attention, and opportunities were always blessed upon her and the family. The others never resented her, nor ever complained of favoritism. How wrong then it would be for me or my colleague to appear in her production alone while brushing the others aside.

The many dawnings of fall

Yes, it does seem that, *for all too soon,* we do grow old and become enlightened far too late. Only now in the early stages of this book, did I come to better understand a possible cause for a very disturbing event from *the troubled years* in summer. [The story was removed from *For all too soon,* as I somehow knew that there was more to one day understand than simple internal pain.] The saga follows on next page; but first, an overture:

Some time ago, a former student, now treasured friend and colleague, sent the link to a well promoted extravaganza video. The program showed another performance in a series about a fine young blind amateur vocalist and pianist. Words like: SHOCKING, DAZZLING, AGAIN, TAKES THE WORLD BY STORM, are sometimes headed up with attention-getting introductions by very creative promoters. This is typical of such things; as in the case of Rebecca, special informative items about the young man in his bio - such as his tutors and learning - were never mentioned. He is autistic, yet talented and musically appealing. However, he has no clue that the promotion puts the focus on him as an anomaly who reached the heights in spite of the fact that he is disabled. He hears the applause, the raving fans, loving comments, but has no way to know that the overwhelming acceptance is influenced by the fact that he is blind and autistic. He has no control over this image, and has no idea that he is an object of commercial marketing.

Now, such *heartless* comments have gotten Richard into trouble on more than one occasion. Folks who are unfamiliar with the blind community in general, will often think the worst of someone who would criticize an event as described above. Yet, intelligent blind people often resent and feel condescended upon by such things. I have actually seen them stand and applaud in the midst of a workshop presentation where such advocacy on their behalf - and for a young artist as described above - was passionately expressed.

Such was the situation described in *For all too soon - Winter*, page 9. The event was during an introductory prologue to a formal school recital. Several blind students convinced me to read a retaliatory spoof on the *ten rules of courtesy when you encounter a blind person*. Well, the reaction of the audience was one of great discomfort, while my blind pranksters hid behind braille programs laughing hysterically. They had set me up knowing what the reaction of the parents would be: poor folks, they felt, who just really *didn't get it*. Now, what "Richard the Cold Hearted" didn't know at the time was, that a parent of two sighted children, later to join the SCCM board, was in attendance. Do read on for the anticlimax.

Amongst the troubled years

The following heartache took place after the complete closure of SCCM teaching facilities, leaving only a small library room soon to close thereafter.

Amongst the many painful events and failures that confronted my colleague, Grant, and me during the troubled years, none pierced my own skin more deeply than a statement made by a new board director who also ... *just didn't get it*.

The last teaching facility was about to close, leaving only the one-room library annex within which to work. I was advised that due to space constrictions and *priorities*, it would not be possible to include computer production equipment needed to provide new braille materials for teaching our blind students. I appealed to several board officials (some were personal friends) to reconsider but was unsuccessful. Once again defeated, I was devastated and felt great despair.

Soon thereafter, I received a hostile email from the new board advisor. Apparently unaware of our long history of make believe scholarships* and mounting personal debts, her opening message read something like: Richard, the shelves are full of braille materials. I think that the reason you won't teach blind students in the library is because you can't be paid.

Having passed all fees charged to schools and colleges for my braille transcription work directly on to SCCM from 1993 to about 2000, the hurt for this one was truly one too many. Invoices had gone out regularly and acquired fees helped to support our braille program such as scholarships, conference costs, supplies, and more. Even close colleagues were not aware of this, as I preferred it that way. With my skin now a bit tougher, I was at least able to avoid another breakdown such as I had experienced after the infamous summons.**

*Make believe scholarships were those where Richard and co-director simply taught for free.

**This story as appearing in *For all too soon* is based on an event that resulted in a complete, but temporary psychological breakdown.

The following (with credits) appears in *For all too soon*, Chapter 26.

The Literacy Movement - What Does Braille Music have to do with it? [1]

When this 1994 article appeared in 'The California Music Teacher' [journal of the Music Teachers' Association of California], *no one could foresee the impending dramatic and rather aggressive demand for academic independence, equality, and career/employment opportunities that would soon overwhelm those of us in the field of music education and visual impairment. This demand would come from those we serve – the blind young people who have refused to remain lost in the 75 (approx.) percent unemployment rate among the blind population. These are the musical few who have learned of published research in music education and brain development – those who now are not afraid to pursue a once often laughed at music diploma, and to brave with confidence, the corporate business world or education and teaching professions. These are the blind young people who KNOW who they are, and that they are unique and special – not in spite of the fact that they are blind – but [often] BECAUSE of it!*[2]

---

[1] Article title appearing in *The California Music Teacher*, Volume 18, Number 1; Fall 1994; content was subject of numerous lectures and conference workshops – referenced here by permission of the author, Richard Taesch.

[2] Excerpt taken from lecture and workshop presented by Richard Taesch at an annual conference for California Transcribers and Educators of the Visually Handicapped – circa 1999 – 2004

What can it all mean?

Prologue - Circa 1977 [revisited with a new purpose]

Early one morning during our pre-class chapel music meeting, Father Phil began to gaze silently toward the large window overlooking upscale homes down slope from the school. Watching him curiously, I waited. Seemingly now removed from the purpose of our conference, he spoke quietly, starring ahead as if in a kind of daydream: "Richard, do you see those large homes in the distance?"

"Yes, Father, I see them."

"This is perhaps one of the most prestigious boys school in the country; here we accept only the highest achievers. They come from wealthy families and work hard to make the *best* grades and graduate with the *highest* honors in order to capture the highest paid careers."

"What's your point, Father?" His gaze remained fixed as he continued:

"They strive to be the very best to gain the most in life; all so that one day they might afford one of ... [hesitatingly] those." He slowly points towards the impressive mansions below then turns towards me: "What possibly can it all mean?"*

*Taken from Outtakes from the back trail - **For all too soon**

As I grow older in my autumn years, questions like *what can it all mean* seem to come up less often. Experiences in life tend to reveal answers in more natural and simple ways. In other words, what it *might* mean seems now to be somewhat irrelevant to why one would ask the question in the first place. For example, I would say that Father Phil, being a fallible human being like the rest of us, surely felt the need to pray for higher enlightenment when perhaps teaching youngsters basic ethics and morality in his early religion classes. If that had not been the case, would he be asking "what possibly can it all mean" at that juncture?

Escape with me now, while I share a few theories or observations of my own.

Robin Hood

Sometimes I think that blaming the rich for our economic and political woes is an escape from failing to solve the more complex issues. The "fat cats" etc., seem to take the blame for everything from climate change to the diminishing number of plies in bath tissue. I'm quite sure that Father Phil was tempted to go there for society misleading the young students in becoming too materialistic. However, he seemed wise enough not to spoil his sudden observation by adding distraction. When I asked "What's your point, Father," what I missed at that time is that he was making his point.

So many tend to forget that, were it not for the rich, such a school would not have students at all! Moreover, the rich pay more than their share in taxes that support less fortunate people. I think that, if anything, *winter* through *summer* taught me to look beyond the obvious. Somewhat summed up in the quote by Mark Twain - paraphrased: *when you find yourself on the side of the majority, it might be time to pause and reflect.*

Sure, there is good and bad in all economic levels of society. However, having spent so many years in the arts and later including visual impairment as an integral part of my career, I can say that if it were not for the rich, Richard's crazy idea of music braille in a music conservatory would not have gotten off the ground at all, much less succeed as it did. *What possibly can it all mean* needs no answer!

Because he wanted to

I once heard that *The Chairman of the Board* (Francis Albert Sinatra) was said to have given more benefit concerts than usual in the year 1979. Although he gave many for children and other causes throughout his career, in '79 they were more frequent.

Apparently unknown to most at the time, in addition to donating his performances, he was said to have absorbed most of the expenses that are usually expected by those promoting such concerts. The question arose as to why would he do that. Why? Because he wanted to! That's why.*

*Inspired by a story told by Jerry Sharell. Radio program: Sharell & Sinatra.

Why is that?

Chapter 2 is a place to ask, explore, and wonder. To dig into contrived conclusions would be no more than distracting and counterproductive to simply stimulating food for thought with possibilities to ponder.

For example, the world cheers each time new satellites are hurled into space. After all, technology is a wonderful thing, including enabling blind musicians to function in a sighted world. However, it does seem that the application of techno is becoming dominated by ... *because we can*, as opposed to ... *how can we make something better*. Techno for the sake of techno seems to be the rule motivating profit without limits, rather than for the betterment of mankind. Have you ever wondered why we would waste valuable spectrum to warm bathwater from one's phone?

There is a website that shows our planet earth and that which surrounds it in orbit. Ambient light from space illuminates each satellite as though stars orbiting the earth. The startling appearance is not unlike a gymnasium decorated for a high school dance. Such is reminiscent of a large crystal sphere that, when a spotlight is pointing at it, emanates as though a planetarium. A good deal of the satellites eventually become defunct and out of service. However, they remain to join more waste, not unlike an overcrowded earthly landfill - a kind of wrecking yard that can't be reached for recycling. They go up in packs for education, GPS, research; but not withstanding are games and the possibility for a student to text his or her comrade sitting within feet in a classroom.

According to one documented source, as of 2021 there were over 6,500 satellites orbiting earth. However, around 3,332 of those are unused, out of service, and have simply become *space junk*! One U.S. agency alone boasts of plans to launch over 40,000 more in coming years. These figures do seem to differ significantly from source to source. *Why is that?*

SHORT STORIES - Points & Views#2

Reality-based fiction (or is it?)

Why do we need that?

My friend and I sat web surfing one evening. I asked him to see if he could *Google* a thing called "Remedial Radiation Belt." I once read that this was (is?) a proposed concept intended to serve as an invisible electronic belt to be launched surrounding the earth. Supposedly, it would then shield our satellites from disturbances caused by sunspot turbulence. The idea did seem to vanish soon thereafter. Objections were raised as to the effects that such a man-made e-belt might have on long distance ionosphere-based communication which depends on sunspot cycles for good radio propagation.* After all, with the Internet, *why do we need that.*(???)

He then suddenly jumped into a site that takes photos of satellites in space. It was quite interesting, indeed. As described earlier, the earth and its orbits appeared like a dance hall sphere surrounded by billions of stars, or perhaps like a skating rink back in the fifties. I mused a bit then said, "John, type in *Remedial Radiation Belt* and see what comes up." We then put in every variation on that name that we could think of and still came up empty - that is until a letter or word was re-worked a bit. When one combination came up that seemed close to RRB that we were looking for, it jumped to a site. The message was: 'Website has been removed.' Perhaps our dance hall green house has found a dual-purpose.

According to radio journal propagation reports, sunspot cycle 24 has not materialized as expected and is late (each cycle should be 11 years long). Long distance direct communication is alarmingly unreliable as of 2019. Why is that?

Invest wisely?

The following story is based on real issues, facts, and places. However, the characters and their situations are fictionalized.

It had been a rather long and tiring legislative session this year, but at last the two aging representatives were now able to sit across from each other at their favorite yearly bistro, sip martinis, and perhaps agree on one or two subjects for a welcome change. They would then fly home to families for less stressful and more routine office duties.

"Phillip, have you given much thought lately on where your investments should be put? Seeing as there are a lot of uncertainties on Wall Street these days, I couldn't help but to wonder." [Jim]

"Well, Jim, I haven't really. But I was reading some interesting money matters a while ago, and it does seem that one needs to more closely watch consumers' rather wasteful priorities that are usually overlooked as virtual goldmines." [Phil]

"Meaning?" [Jim]

"Well, take for example the mobile devices that we discard and update as often as our underwear, and the units that power them - chargers, batteries, etc. Last year's model would most likely serve much longer, but apps and updates from providers render them obsolete even before our underwear wear out!" [Phil]

"So what's your point, Phil?" [Jim]

"Think about it. Each updated device requires an updated battery and matching charger." Phil responds, in a slightly elevated tone. [Phil]

"Guess this martini is too strong, as I still don't get it." [Jim]

"OK: invest in lithium mines, as most battery applications rely on them and chargers must match that application. *Stock Market 101* strongly supports that approach. The more updates, the more profit. Quite simple, I think." [Phil]

"But, Phil, if it's illegal to toss a dead lithium battery in the dumpster, or even to mail a device that uses one, shouldn't we give some thought to the moral or ecological side of things; you know, the kinda' green thing?" [Jim]

"Why? No one would make any money that way!" grins Phil, sipping, while staring out of one eye towards his puzzled comrade. "After all, you must have problems in order to create profits." [Phil]

"Hmmm; in other words, whether you support border walls or not, invest in cement?" [Jim]

"Exactly!" [Phil]

The geography lesson

"Geography books on desks, please! Turn to page 7." clamored the teacher while students were still settling into studies following lunch hour. It had been another chilly Nebraska day, and Ms. Jeffries felt that reading about a place with a tropical type of climate might be fun for the winter-weary children.

"I'm going to summarize the highlights of the lesson, so no need to read just yet. Homework will follow based upon the reading from this chapter. I will leave some specific facts out; take note of each now. You are to fill them in from your reading." [1]

"There is only one inland sea in North America; it lies in a great desert that was once part of the ocean. Dried up for perhaps centuries, it reformed in 1906 due to an accidental diversion of the Colorado River resulting in over 400 square miles of sea. It is sometimes called a lake, but has no outlets; therefore, it is not a lake, but a true salt water *sea* by definition.

"During the mid 1900s, it became known as the__ (name of a state?)_____ *Riviera*, as boaters, fishermen, water sports enthusiasts, and celebrities swarmed to its shores. Warm temperatures all year round attracted people from everywhere. Investors and land promoters poured money into the area. Bird migrations from South America all the way to the Arctic Circle came to depend upon this sea, creating national and international ecological ramifications.

"Towards the end of the 1970s, flooding from agriculture runoff and an unexpected hurricane began the demise of the great _____ Sea. Resorts closed, hotels and business abandoned the area, and a military base closed. Some new marinas and yacht clubs maximized the change, excavating new inlets at a higher water level. The flood waters then began to recede in the 1980s, leaving the new sea once again in ruins.

"Not all is hopeless, as plans to revive the 100 miles of shoreline development are in place; but unfortunately, always being delayed. Due to reasons perhaps only known to politicians, other priorities could potentially doom the only last remaining wetland on the _____Flyway to extinction."

Some children's eyes began filling with tears as Ms. Jeffries continued: "Sea birds are dying by the millions and massive fish die offs are common. Toxic dust storms from exposed seabed reach across the entire state and beyond. The last nail in that coffin is a plan to divert even more river water from the desert to an ocean side city, where desalinization could be a possible option.

"Indian reservations border the shores of the _____ Sea where casinos that are legal could put life-saving funds into restoration of their home. A major desert resort city, once a Mecca for celebrities, lies within minutes of the sea. Yet it appears authorities would rather fund less important projects, while launching and ignoring another of the worst ecological catastrophes of the last two centuries."

Salton Bay Yacht Club in ruins - 1985

Salton Bay Yacht Club - ca. 1970

[1.] Look for the missing facts hidden somewhere in or near a later chapter. Hint: Richard may be living at the sea by time this sequel has been published. The keywords will not be underlined.

III

So you want to be a music teacher!

As I reflect back on a long and fruitful life as a music teacher, so many humorous and unique situations come to mind that are worth sharing. Not all were funny at the time, but having survived the smart phone demons, their uniqueness is like a precious gem to be passed on to teachers, students, and parents - who, by the way, have all earned my deepest respect and honor!

Outtakes from the back studio

It was a typical busy evening at the original conservatory headquarters. Lessons were going on in every teaching room while ensembles and teachers rehearsed in the two larger areas. Each time a teaching module door opened, the area would sound like tuning sessions at the philharmonic prior to the conductor's downbeat.

The school director rarely paid much attention to room schedules, or whether any room at all was available for faculty use. So, in struts Mr. Straybrass - late as usual, violin case in hand, out of breath, and hoping his make-up student wouldn't notice him sneaking in the back door. Available rooms for lessons were generally not a problem. He would simply snag an empty one (he thought), quickly set up shop and proceed to waltz out to the waiting area looking at his watch as if to say,

"Loretta, you're late again; tsk, tsk." Well, not this time! The clock was ticking as the student became nervous, wondering if her maestro would show up at all.

Meanwhile, our *Paganini* frantically searches for an open teaching room. There were none. Suddenly, he spots the only way out of this mess. In typical - *don't ask questions; what else do you expect at this conservatory* - style, he seizes the opportunity like a kitten dashing for a plate of food amongst its siblings. He opens the door of the "convenience" and grabs a single folding chair stored in the shower. He then pops down the lid for his distinguished teaching position, opens a music stand, summons Loretta, and the very late lesson finally commences. (Oh yes, this actually happened; honestly.)

* * *

If there was one thing that Dr. Maur cherished about having his own private teaching studio, it was the luxury of a back room well furnished with coffee maker, refrigerator, and a cushy little cot for naps while waiting for students to beckon at lesson times. Of course, not all students that the distinguished professor was gifted to teach were stellar; thus the purpose of the cot behind the screen.

Late as usual, in *boogies* Jorge, perhaps the most difficult piano student to challenge any teacher at staying awake during his lesson. Jorge never practiced, and always forgot at least one piece of music; usually the least prepared one.

Professor and subject under tutelage now take their seats and the lesson begins. Well, about three measures into the minuet, Maur's eyelids begin to quiver. He kindly says: "Keep playing, Jorge. I'm going into my kitchen and make a cup of coffee. I'll be listening from there and we'll do comments when I return in about five minutes."

So young *Mozart* continues to play the first short movement and waits. No Dr. Maur yet. He again bungles through the ill-prepared work; no Dr. Maur; no smell of brewing coffee. About fifteen minutes goes by and the boy really becomes worried that something has happened to his beloved teacher. He quietly gets up, wanders towards the forbidden sanctuary, gently pulls aside the drape and there lays maestro snoring in heavenly peace, ZZZZzzzzzz...

The following was later found on Dr. Maur's bulletin board in the student waiting room:

NOTICE TO STUDENTS:
[Reprint from *For all too soon*]

You really can help prevent your teacher from falling asleep during your lesson by coming prepared.

If this is not possible, kindly make arrangements with other students scheduled before or after your lesson time to come somewhat prepared on alternate weeks. In this way, your teacher need only remain conscious for every other lesson.

Your cooperation is greatly appreciated. Thank you!

* * *

I was quite young when I began as a student teacher. I soon realized that not even the image reflected by means of a dress coat and tie would save me from rookie duties such as going to students' homes for lessons contracted by the music academy. Once becoming a "senior" neophyte, that gig could be passed off to other new, and less experienced trainees. Nonetheless, the families of the kids were always wonderful and welcomed me into their homes, most of which were usually in upscale communities.

This particular day, my car was still tied up in the repair shop as it came close to time for a home lesson at 4pm. A friend was kind enough to drop me off at the shop to pick up my car which was to be ready. It was not. Drat! Now what do I do? Well, the owner of the shop expressed great sympathy and apologized profusely as though that would fix everything.

"Richard, I think I have a solution, uh, but ..."

"But?"

"Well, we aren't using that tow truck sitting there; and, uh, why don't you just drive yourself to your appointment in that. You can drop it off here tomorrow when you come to pick up your car which should be ready by then."

I slowly turned around to look and there it was - complete with *Acme Towing* in large red letters that adorned the white painted doors. This was not a car carrier, but the old type of tow hitch and wench, not unlike a tractor for a commercial truck trailer - emergency lights on the roof and all the trimmings!

Sensing my fright, Mel says: "You'll do fine, Richard, just don't play with all those levers near the shifter on the floor. It'll be fun; honest!"

"Mel, fun is what I don't need! I just need to get to work and not pull up looking like I'm about to tow an illegally parked car in, of all places, Beverly Hills!"

"Now, now; just chill out! Perhaps you'd rather walk there. Count your [as he clears his throat] blessings, and get your musical ass on the road or you'll be late! Now be gone with you."

Pulling up to the house was probably worth the price of admission! Drapes opened, kids and parent peered out while Mr. Taesch and his coat, tie, guitar case, and clipboard began waltzing up to the door as if he drove a tow truck to their lessons every week. Waiting to give an explanation upon opening the door, I simply winked and said: "Well, I thought it was a good idea just in case my car broke down again. Besides, it's April Fool's Day tomorrow."

* * *

RICHARD E. TAESCH

SHORT STORIES - Points & Views #3
Of course we need that!

Of course we need that. Why? Because we care about kids, that's why!

As explained in *For all too soon,* music teachers in the private sector have a rather unique vista. As said: "A family may raise one or many children, watching them only once through each growth period to adulthood. A private music teacher in perhaps a fifty-year career, has seen students that attend for extended periods through thousands of such changes. In addition, he or she has had an enhanced vista of every different personality imaginable, as well as many family ethnic and economic backgrounds to compare them to." This sensitivity extends to all kids in our flock and well beyond.

It was early in the 1990s, and I was hiking high in the San Gabriel Mountains with a commanding view of peaks far off to the northeast. Suddenly, the appearance and smell of smoke hovering above the peaks in my view monopolized my full attention. Although not close enough at this time to be a threat, the view of large water-dropping aircraft confirmed the stark reality of a growing forest fire.

The time was well before cell phones and such but as an Amateur Radio operator, I generally carried a small hand-held transceiver with me. Out came the radio, and soon the Blue Ridge repeater came alive with volunteer operators manning a command post. The activity appeared to be monitoring the progress of a mandatory evacuation of scouts from an endangered summer camp.

I was able to hear both stations clearly as they struggled to copy each other in the effort to direct an emergency bus to the camp for a rescue. The stations were unable to confirm directions, as mountains blocked a clear signal. I listened intensely, waiting to see if acknowledgment between them could be made. The fire was growing, and the camp was now in grave danger.

Breaking into the communication hoping that both stations could hear me even though they could not hear each other, I offered: "This is K6TOB; may I QSP on your behalf?" [QSP indicates a Q Code message to act as a relay in such situations.]

"Yes, please! Where are you?"

"Near Blue Ridge, perhaps 10 miles to your southwest."

At that point, I was able to relay the directions from the command post to the station communicating with the vehicle. The kids were successfully evacuated and safely taken out of danger.

Yes, there are many who feel that the Internet has replaced the need for licensed over-the-air communication. *Of course we need that. Why? Because we care about kids, that's why!*

Which way from where?

Those who teach music often have friends and colleagues who may share many of the same hobbies and avocations. My long time friend and fellow jazz musician, Fred, also loved to hike. He taught Richard much about backpacking as well as being an occasional trail companion. Fred was also a scout master at one time, and organized a student backpacking club at the high school where he taught for many years.

One day while on one of our favorite day hikes, I told him the following little story about the same area that we were in at the moment and about a lost scout master with a group of kids. It certainly got his attention! He shook his head and proceeded to recite - with a tone of experience - what "not to do" when responsible for leading any hike. [Story follows]

Hiking alone in the Mt. Pinos wilderness, I was on my way back towards my trailhead as it was nearing dark. Suddenly, I spotted what appeared to be a troop of boy scouts poring over a trail map along with their scoutmaster. "Hmm," I thought; "wonder if they're lost?" Cautiously, not wanting to alarm the boys to lose confidence in their leader, I avoided the word *lost* and just said: "Hello; where have you fellows been? - must've been fun."

The scout leader, looking somewhat sheepish but relieved, asked if I'd take a look at his map to spot a point of interest. Moving out of earshot of the kids, he told me that they were on their way to a trail camp called *Sheep Camp*, but not sure how far they had to go. They were planning to camp there for the night. He was obviously a bit shaken, as he had become confused to directions.

By this time I knew that they were clearly heading the wrong way, and that I had caught them just in time. Dark was about 30 minutes away, and their fate was perhaps one that could have spoiled the trip. So again, without alarming the kids, I directed him to take the other trail and that the Sheep Camp turnoff would be about 3 miles on their left. Wiping his sweaty brow, *Daniel Boone* addresses the kids in a new found confident *scout master* tone: "OK kids! Saddle up and we go that way!"

"Oh, by the way, sir," I added: "Do you have flashlights, as it'll be dark well before you are able to set up camp?"

"Of course; you didn't think we would come here unprepared, did you?" as he winked at me and firmly shook hands.

The following week, Fred led a short hike of school kids in a new state park across the canyon from where I live. I didn't join them this time, but I had introduced Fred to that trail sometime before. Sitting in my front room practicing that morning while sipping coffee, I was able to peer across to the mountain quite far away with my trusty binoculars. In full view of the ridge trail where I knew I would spot them, there goes scout leader Fred, team, and all frantically bush-whacking on a different ridge, obviously having lost the trail altogether.

Later after what must have been a successful recovery, I informed him that I had witnessed the whole pageant from afar, describing the scene as it appeared.

"So Fred, what was it you told me that a leader should *not do* when ..."

"Never mind!"

> *The following edited excerpt is based upon an extended article describing a familiar dilemma that braille music transcribers often face while trying to conform to copyright laws. [With permission]*

What about the student?

SCENERIO: A young student (first chair) is fully involved in a fine high school orchestra and band program. Director *Dizzy*, as expected, has provided a dozen tattered, tiny marching-band-sized and scribbled-upon charts to the DSS office to be transcribed into braille. It is Friday, and music rehearsals begin on Monday!

Now before we orchestrate further upon this somewhat familiar pedagogical headache, and before we become entertained by what the braille transcriber must be thinking, let us consider a few highlights.

The rules from the copyright section (statements for preliminary braille pages) [omitted here] found in Formats 2016, list the requirements that transcribers must conform to. [Copyright laws require non-affiliated (independent) transcribers to obtain publisher's permission **before** beginning any transcription.]

OK! Now it's time for a pop-quiz in order to see just how you - the transcribers - conform to protocol and how we should proceed to solve this age-old problem.

MULTIPLE CHOICE:

Given the information in the *Scenario* described above, the music transcriber is required to apply which of the following procedures BEFORE beginning the transcription of this student's music [it's Friday, and all is due by Monday]:

1. Recommend that the student drop orchestra class for one year, or at least until you have obtained permission from each of the 12 publishers
2. Report the school to the Attorney General for not obtaining authorization to reproduce copyrighted works
3. If the copyright notices are illegible or photocopied off of the page, you must research the government database to find the titles in question first, then proceed as required
4. Begin work, as copyright clearance does not apply to us
5. Require the band director to learn music transcription
6. Ignore the rule just like everyone else
7. Open a beer, then lie down until the worry goes away
8. Get even with Dr. Dizzy by reporting him for distributing photo copies of copyrighted music
9. Join the growing "Me Too" movement of retiring music transcribers
10. Become comfortable with working illegally

The answer to the above quiz indicated that: ... *Number 1 might fly, but then* **what about the student?**

A short tale of Roland the shrink

Dr. Roland, sitting patiently in the waiting area for his weekly guitar lesson, sat sporting his new permanent curly hairdo. Apparently, it was more practical for when he would enjoy his hobby of hot air ballooning.

Guitar teacher, Richard, running late as usual, finally opens the studio door for the exchange of subjects, apologizes profusely:

"Yo, Roll! I'm really sorry, but things just got out of hand and, well, you know. I just can't stop a lesson when he doesn't understand something."

"Oh, man! No problem." Roland exclaims quietly, as though about to impart a classified secret: "You've got to learn to do what I do in such situations."

"What?"

"I just open the door to my patient room closing it behind me. I say to my next patient: 'Charlie, I'm sorry to be running late but you are doing so well in your therapy that I thought you wouldn't mind; but this poor guy in there is really having big problems, and I need about twenty minutes more with him. Hope you can understand.'"

Yes, what about the student?

I've been a long time advocate in the cause for music literacy and blind college students. In addition to being their music transcriber, I often found myself in a multi-sided role of consultant, student & instructor liaison, and tutor. One rather unique and intriguing example follows.

It soon became quite clear to me that the music department faculty were doing their best to discourage young Diana. They seemed very uncomfortable with the thought of making adjustments to curricula for this particular blind student. Perhaps her outspoken persona, and being already somewhat of an accomplished vocalist, may have simply appeared overly assertive to them. Nonetheless, conferences with the primary professors revealed nothing less than a rough road ahead for her.

My first meeting with the Disabilities Support Services (DSS) before the semester began seemed highly constructive. We discussed long term plans for Diana's schooling such as how materials in braille would be handled, turnaround time, costs, and alternate media specialist interaction.

Of primary concern with faculty was handling of testing, quizzes, and *assumed* complexities that might confront them due to her special needs. I assured them that they would not be burdened or distracted from normal protocol. They should simply view her as they would any other student and let me worry about the rest. They only needed to refer to DSS should any problems arise.

Our first semester seemed unusual in that private assistants were assigned to her, resulting in what appeared to be an accelerated program usually reserved for highly gifted students. Chapter after chapter from the primary music theory textbook came to me for transcription in, what I felt, was an unprecedented rate. Where most music majors would normally complete one or two chapters per week, three or four were arriving for me to complete every few days!

The pace of theory and harmonic analysis material being covered, along with vocal and other choral repertoire in braille, was no less than overwhelming for us to keep up with as being demanded. As a result, Diana would call me at my home; we would spend hours in tutorial and help sessions. As luck would have it, along with chasing this "brass ring" that could not be caught, I was called for a complex and lengthy jury duty trial then became ill. Nonetheless, I continued to work for her to meet their seemingly unreasonable demands at the same time. Something was not right, but neither of us recognized what, other than the fact that Diana was not at all being treated as would any other student. The trial finally ended late on Christmas Eve, with no holiday spirit for me or for the student.

As winter classes continued at this furious pace, my own school began to tumble in the 2008 economic debacle. I was turning braille theory chapters around without being able to proofread any of them. The situation worsened until Diana *threw in her towel* and dropped out of the university program for a full year.

However, not all is dismal. As Calvin Coolidge once wrote something like: ... *only perseverance is omnipotent,* Diana returned one year later determined to get the education that she deserved. Read on, as there is a very happy ending to come.

Diana re-enrolled in the university program, but again was greeted with a rather cool attitude from the same professors. Another pre-entry conference was arranged. This time the student was formally invited to attend along with myself, DSS Chair, and several disappointed and defensive professors.

As the meeting opened, a faculty spokesman demanded that Diana leave the room, as she should not be present to inhibit their candid discussions. Objections were expressed by DSS but to no avail.

I sat, thought, and calmly said to myself: "Richard, remember Rebecca and the many others that you had to defend their right to music literacy. Stand up to them! Dramatize if you have to, but whatever you do, remember the saga of the clipboard and remember your own words: *Not this time you don't. This is her shining moment, and not you or anyone else is going to take that from her!*"

I saw the fear and bad karma in their eyes and in the words of the teachers. Suddenly I softened inside. I began to pity their unfounded feelings and felt the opportunity to neutralize this negative demon, turn them around, and hope for the best.

Well, before the meeting was over we became aligned and good colleagues! They were grateful for my firmness and for enlightening them. Diana was warmly welcomed back into the program, and even though a few bumpy roads were yet to be navigated, she graduated with honors and went on to make all proud by being accepted into the Royal Academy in the UK for continuing study!

By the way, the trial turned out *not guilty* of DUI for a young and very frightened piano tuner! So yes, winning can sometimes be the right thing for everyone. *Fighting is never good; someone always gets hurt. But if one must fight, WIN!* (Loosely paraphrased: *The Karate Kid.*)

RICHARD E. TAESCH

IV

Summer memories

Among *the many summer memories* that Richard will carry throughout his fall, is the rare privilege of seeing "Old Blue Eyes" (Frank Sinatra) live in concert! It was in the early 1980s and quite late in his career. My young lady friend following my divorce was able to purchase tickets for the concert at the Universal Amphitheater. Drummer Buddy Rich conducted his big band behind Frank, while Tony Mattola provided guitar work for duet performances.

Coming from a younger generation, Victoria was not all that familiar with Sinatra and his music, but knew my desire to see him. She made very special efforts to surprise me, and indeed I was very surprised and overwhelmed! The program focused on the 1965 album, *September of My Years,* as this time was truly the *autumn* of his years. I couldn't help but to quietly notice that my friend was rather pensive throughout the performance, yet extremely attentive and silent - not unlike one who has seen the Grand Canyon for the first time.

She had been to see a current pop rock artist at the same amphitheater one week before, and commented that she was a little disappointed in the fact that the artist spent significant time injecting political innuendos throughout her performance.

Following the concert, we began to exit the theater through a foyer. During the slow exodus, some of Frank's album - *September of My Years* - was playing as atmosphere above our heads. The crowd was rather quiet during the recession toward the doors, almost as if entranced by the whole experience.

Suddenly, Victoria began to show tears in her eyes then quietly began sobbing. She stopped, and we sat together momentarily on benches in the hallway. I waited and watched for a moment, somewhat puzzled, but not sure if I dare ask what ... - she then began to speak:

"Richard, that man doesn't need the money for that performance. He showed no ego or greatness to fulfill, and yet - she continued even more tearfully - he gave his heart and all the love he could for those who had paid to see him sing. It seemed that was all that mattered in his life."

"Well, Victoria, that's the soul of a great artist; Frank was always like that."

Apparently, generation gap or not, she was so deeply moved by something she had never experienced before, that she was simply overwhelmed. Old Blue Eyes lived to please his fans until about 1993 which, as I understand, was his last concert. At 83 years *young at heart*, he left us in 1998.

***

***Those who have read* "For all too soon"** may remember a story about one of Richard's favorite bistros, that of *Georgio's* in Palm Springs. It opened with a statement like: "How does one describe Georgio's? Where does one begin?" Although not as well known amongst the desert elite, Van Nuys California was the home of a quaint little diner called *Slim's Eat a Burger*. It was nestled on a modest little side street, just convenient enough to attract many Federal building folks, business owners, as well as the music teachers at the *Center of Music* just around the corner.

Slim's was quite reminiscent of the Edward Hopper poster of a similar diner named *Phillies* hanging in The Art Institute of Chicago. The counter scene - two patrons as seen at night from the back through the outside window, the chef going about his duties dressed in the usual white clothing and chef's hat, might even bring a deep sigh from those who frequented the place. Slim once said, "It's sad that kids now have never experienced a real malted milk or a real hamburger." And how right he was, as the food was simple but ingredients and preparation were of the finest that could be found anywhere!

All of the patrons came to know each other, as day to day they would take their places on the little round stools at the counter, perhaps no longer than fifteen or twenty feet total. Slim would prepare a huge caldron of his homemade chili weekly. Customers would walk in, and the usual playful insults such as: "Hey Keith; when did they let you out?" etc. would be no less than funny no matter how many times one would hear it. Keith was a retired postman who had delivered mail to my home nearby when I was perhaps no more than twelve years old. He even delivered my first novice Amateur Radio license in about 1956. Now on crutches, he would not likely remember me. All of the patrons were regulars; probably lifetime residents of the beautiful little town that Van Nuys was at one time.

Slim's own history was no less than fascinating. On slow days he would enjoy sharing it with those of us who were successful at starting him to chat. For example, before opening his little diner as it stood at this time, he was a "hasher" at the *Chili Burger,* then located adjacent to the Burbank airport runway. He claimed that he was working there on the day that Amelia Earhart took off on her famous flight, but never returned.

One street to the south of where I lived after divorce, and near where I grew up in Van Nuys, was a street called Sylvan Street. Slim told of the days sometime in the thirties or forties when actor Clark Gable would take a bus from Hollywood to Van Nuys to visit his girlfriend who lived on Sylvan. On his way, he would stop at Slim's to have a nickel cup of coffee. As I understood the story, she was the only woman that Gable was alleged to have had a child with.

Slim's beautiful white 1958 *Coup de Ville* sat proudly outside the back door of *Eat a Burger*. Today there is no evidence of the Cadillac or the simple wholesome food that was once a treasured icon of true

Americana. Slim was as proud of his car as he was the food that he served. Such things as they were known to be then are mostly extinct in 2019.

So long, Slim; *for all too soon,* you were gone.

* * *

SHORT STORIES - Points & Views #4
Faces of evil

> The title, *Faces of evil,* in the following stories does not pertain to the characters themselves. I have come to believe - through many painful experiences - that demons do exist! Their energy can influence us and our fellow beings in many ways, including greed and power, or even unintentional abuse.

The legacy

Clearly, not all of our autumn memories are pleasant ones. Nonetheless, they are part of us and, as said before, a part of where we have been and where we must go. The following is the true story of an acquaintance known as Jed.

Following a devastating divorce, Jed was left with little in the way of savings, and felt that he would never own a home again. Making matters worse, the neighborhood around the quaint duplex that he occupied began to deteriorate, leaving break-ins a common occurrence.

Unexpectedly, a miracle of sorts came out of hiding and Jed was somehow able to purchase a trailer home in a wonderful community known to him as, *nirvana.*

Time went by. Just like the closing of Slim's Eat a Burger, nirvana became virtual and no longer the real thing. A corporation took over, landscapers were let go, street sweepers and tree trimmers were no more.

Rents soared, leaving many home owners little choice but to abandon their properties. The miracle of Jed's nirvana became not unlike a rundown slum ruled by a ruthless corporate mind - profit became its Goddess.

By this time, Jed's rent had increased from pre-corporate times to near $500 per month more! With a heavy heart, he sat down to write the president of the investment group the following letter:

Dear Ms. Ambig - CEO, Properties Investor Group - PIG:

I am writing to you in response to our annual rent increase. Kindly take a moment to read my thoughts, those of one who has enjoyed it here for nearly thirty years - perhaps one of the happiest homes that l have ever had.

Nonetheless, since your group has taken over here, the feeling for me is that of one who is pulling a heavy cart uphill while someone else keeps adding more and more weight to it.

I'm 75 years old on fixed SSA, and must continue to work into retirement in order to meet that endlessly increasing weight, all so as not to lose my home. My own eyes are becoming weaker as a result and this work may not be possible much longer.

PIG has brought nothing but resentment, anger, and run down conditions to this once beautiful community and levied unreasonable increases in exchange; the park has become so unsightly that I'm almost ashamed to invite guests here. My neighbor who will be 85 next month wears an overcoat all winter to reduce heating costs, all to meet the corporation's insatiable appetite.

No, I'm not asking for anything! I simply needed to share the deepening sadness and a feeling of hopelessness. Ms. Ambig, I am perhaps old enough to be your grandfather! And I must say – as I would to a child or one of my own kids – that, if this is the legacy you are willing to take into your own later years, be *very* sure that you are ready to own it, and to live with it.

Sincerely,
Jed, Space #97

The letter was sent by certified mail; to this day as to my knowledge, no response was ever been received by Jed.

The investor

Richard's short experimental escapade in the Real Estate world never produced much in the way of financial gain. However, his own investment in how he observes the world of some business ethics could fill a novel on its own merit.

Just when I was about to exit the project as *enough*, I was assigned to a client that seemed quite willing to stay with me until he found the property that he wanted. At this point, I had no idea that his purpose was not to find his dream home, but that of "flipping" a property of good value in a very bad market. I showed him several potential listings; he then latched on to one he liked and was determined to acquire it. He had done his homework and knew that the owner was motivated, as he was near desperate to sell with foreclosure looming.

We looked over the property several times during our weekly tours of new listings. Each time, the house would drop in listed price. This particular day, he indicated that he was now going to make an offer. We once again visited the home, studied the MLS (Multiple Listing Service), and went to lunch. I fully expected to go back to my office with him to write the offer as he had led me to believe.

As we sat chatting following another fine lunch on my credit card, I asked him if he planned to close the deal. I never used the "closure" technique on any client, and avoided any hint of pressure with all of the folks that I had worked with (probably why I never made the million seller list). As we continued to chat over a pleasant cup of coffee, he revealed his true colors. He was a professional real estate investor who would only seek desperate sellers near ruin. He would then move in fast, not unlike a wild predator that picks out the weakest prey in a flock and knows that he will make a sure kill.

"Well, Jerry," I said as I paid the lunch bill, "what do you think?"

"Nope! I'm going to wait a little longer and watch to see if any offers come in. I want to squeeze him until he bleeds."

The next day I tried to contact Jerry but he was nowhere to be found. He had moved in on his own, cutting my commission that would have been. He then acquired the property at the "bottom line" in a foreclosure sale.

Richard's Real Estate career ended soon after that, but he walked away from it having gained a major fortune in experience and how to recognize betrayal even in his own music profession.

The betrayal

Ricardo worked behind the scenes of his career most of his life. A lifelong music teacher in the private, conservatory, and some college sectors, he went quietly about his work day to day avoiding administrative duties as much as possible.

For many years, Ricardo taught primarily in rented studios and enjoyed the pride of carrying a waiting list for those seeking his work. Students came and went. In one music school where he headed the department, he had gathered quite a few students that stayed with him for many years - some from pre-teen to becoming college graduates. One young man was particularly a favorite to Ricardo and made him quite proud on many a school recital over the years. They came to be somewhat of buddies as well, and gatherings with Peter's family would sometimes include his teacher.

Peter was now nearing 17 years of age and preparing for a special performance quite crucial to Ricardo's work at the school. *Crucial* in that, poor economic times had rendered his enrollment quite low. As such, he was planning to enter the boy in a special teachers' association venue in hopes to revive his ailing department. Peter had reached a young artist level and, although never one to *blow his own horn* as a celebrity teacher, Ricardo felt that Peter just might be the catalyst to turn the tide at this point in his troubled career.

One afternoon while bringing the boy to his lesson, mom stopped to have an important discussion with his teacher.

She expressed that they would be stopping lessons in a month as, having just moved, the weekly drive had become a hardship. Perhaps he would return once he were to get his own car. She said that he was broken hearted, and so much appreciated all Ricardo had done for him over the years.

Speechless and choking deep inside, Ricardo responded: "Arlene, I truly understand and much appreciate the difficulty that you must have had preparing to tell me."

The following week as innocence goes, Peter let it slip: they had been working covertly for over a month with a new teacher who was a performing musician with many credits. Peter's reason for revealing this was so that - he felt - Ricardo would feel confident that he was in capable hands and not to worry.

Mom came in for Peter's last lesson proudly showing posters, promotional literature, and pictures of Mr. Carlos. Ricardo sat at his computer quietly, never looking up at Arlene. "Ricardo," she asked, "what time is the special recital this Saturday as it's our final goodbye?"

"For what, Arlene? I'm sorry, but my work gave life and breath to Peter's musical development while Senior Carlos will now take credit for it on his next recital. There will be no further performances with me, as for the last four weeks he was not my student!"

Clearly, Ricardo would have been willing to meet Mr. Carlos and to support the family's need to relocate Peter's studies; but he now felt that the privilege was denied him, and that he had been betrayed.

"Arlene, I feel that I should have at least had the chance to tell the man of Peter's background of ten years with me. I would have been proud to shake Mr. Carlos's hand and pass the boy on to him with dignity. I was being deceived while you hid the truth from me."

True, that Ricardo's technique was not what it once was due to a disability, and that Carlos was a dazzling and impressive player; but as a young teacher, his lack of time and experience could not compare. Ricardo may never completely come to peace with the truth and will always feel betrayed even though in his heart, he still believes that the family only meant well, and never to purposefully dishonor him.

It's NOT free

While separating food stamps items from those not eligible at the check stand, the following exchange between a graying shopper and the young man checker commenced just one day before Thanksgiving holiday:

'OK; let's get the *free* stuff done first" states the checker in a somewhat authoritative and arrogant tone.

Having become just impatient enough with fogged up glasses from Covid masks, grating comments from a smart ass cashier, rotten onions from the last trip at this same store, the response to that rather untimely and ill-placed command - while startled customers in line stared in a dense pall that engulfed the moment - was:

"Son! It's NOT free!" Looking the boy straight in the eye and pointing directly at him, he continued gently: "I've been paying into this system probably before your parents were born. Moreover, most of us will never live long enough to use up the benefits blessed upon those of us in need - blessed by the people of this great country that you and I should be proud to be living in! Now may I suggest that you go and read about the Great Depression, then fall to your knees and give thanks."

V

Reflections

Some of the stories in *Summer's Memory* could have been included within time frames in *For all too soon*. But with all of the history, ups and downs, troubled and good years, I felt that many eventualities here were simply not appropriate there. They needed to mature in my mind and to have their own time and space. With all of its blessings and heartaches, my first remembrance needed to have an overall feeling for me of triumph. Wonder, and that marvelous tone of "magic" was always in the air in spite of struggles and tears. Goodness, love, and perseverance were always the theme. The word *practical* was never a deterrent!

I truly believe that my stories and experiences are not mine alone. Situations and outcomes between us may differ but, my dear reader, do try to walk with me in this part of my life. If you can put yourself into the characters and times, you may even see your own image in many similar *reflections*. Such is unavoidable, as you are also a striving human being walking under the same sun.

Reflections from the back trails of our minds

Attending weddings can be fun even as a guest when not part of the band that is playing for the event. Jan and April had been long time friends, and both were professional performers in their own rite: Jan, a musician, composer, and dancer; April, a working actress since childhood. This time, I was an invited guest to celebrate Jan's wedding. She was marrying a talented guitarist and composer who had also been a former student of mine.

Following the ceremonies, the reception began lasting well into the night. As I stood chatting with a drink in my hand, the crowd suddenly went into hysterical laughter and cheering. What, where, who, were all tossing about my mind as I tried to gather what was happening. There it was, bigger than life: April and a cohort running butt naked across the auditorium - in from one door and quickly disappearing out of another. A wedding gift or *streaks* of genius, one will never know; but an event that will always remain a highlight of Jan's special day it was! Now the streaking craze had somewhat faded, but there is more to come. Do read on.

Sometime later, April was celebrating her life as an actress. Many friends had gathered to put on a very special event for her. It was to help raise funds for April and a very serious life-threatening illness. I had volunteered to help with setting up and so forth. Mostly, I was asked to play in a small combo so as to back April for her performance singing some of her compositions as a surprise for the guests. Jan's new husband was playing bass and I was on guitar. Throughout the day we were informed that there would be a special happening at about 4pm - even the band didn't know the secret. However, we were to play a fanfare of sorts once the mystery event commenced.

This was, quite coincidentally, Richard's last time to perform publicly after 40 years of gigs. Yes, he was "hanging up his guns" after a life of gigs and band stories, other than some performances with students in recitals.

Suddenly, the familiar sound of laughter and fun that was at Jan's wedding became evident. From across the hall in *I'll get you back* style, came Jan running, dashing alone while wearing nothing but a smile. She then disappeared out of a door - not to be seen until later as though nothing such had ever happened. April passed as a result of her illness in 2003.

* * *

Long before I decided to quit gigging, I worked many union jobs in the seventies. But for many musicians, there were never enough to go around. Some resigned from the locals and managed to work for less money, but at least there was always some simple casual band work that kept them going. Others would "ride the fence," so to speak, working with or without the blessings of their union.

Mike was a daytime school teacher, but also depended on cash income from the dance band work he took on. He was a brilliant saxophone player, and would often gig on the docked merchant ship, *Princess Louise*. If one was a union member, it was always quite a skill to work incognito. Often, the reps would slip in to see if they could catch a culprit working without reporting the job to the local. Sidemen were quite used to never giving actual names, leaders' names, and would even go so far as wearing wigs to disguise themselves. Avoiding strangers looking to chat was always a must, as they were often undercover agents.

This particular gig, Mike was on a break to visit the *convenience*, as the beer was nagging at him a bit. As he was standing attending to business, in walks a fellow taking his place next to him. While the evacuation was progressing, the stranger said in a warm and friendly way: Great band you have there. Who's the leader?

Mike declares: "Gee thanks! It's Jay Conner's band. Here's my card" as he hands the fellow his own card proudly displaying his name and instrument.

"Oh thanks! Here is mine." They zipped, shook hands, and the spy was gone.

In big letters with a union logo, the gentleman's name card was followed by *Field Representative - Musicians Union*. --Gotcha'!

SHORT STORIES - Points & Views #5

Lockhart revisited

Prologue: The news was meant to be quite uplifting, as energy consumption would now have another monetary incentive to expand in the Mojave Desert of California. The radio newscaster, placing emphasis on the urgent need to meet the ever growing demand of customers, enthusiastically described a planned expansion of an existing solar city in the desert.

It does seems to me that, at times, we are more encouraged to applaud the growing technology that provides for consuming more and more as opposed to when enough is enough. As mentioned earlier, do we really need to produce more wattage so as to prepare bathwater from our phones? Or perhaps electric vehicles capable of four hundred horsepower might certainly justify the need for new grants. After all, we must produce more energy so as to power larger charging devices for such *necessary* toys. (??)

I suppose that my thirst for such things was somewhat diminished when, on one fine Thanksgiving Day, I walked into my longtime friends' home having been invited for festivities. The table was set to perfection. The smell of cooking turkey filled the air stirring memories of when I was once married with a family of my own. Board games in readiness, coffee, and dessert always topped off the tradition with delight.

As I walked into the dining room, the familiar countertop serving area - once adorned with family photos, memoirs, candy dishes, other holiday things - had been replaced with seven charging devices. Tablets and smart phones waiting their turn for a charge, appeared like jets lined up for their turn on the runway. I suddenly entered a momentary state of quiet sadness. It was as though I had awakened from a holiday fantasy into the world of digital virtual reality. I carefully hid my letdown from deep inside, smiled, and greeted the other guests.

RICHARD E. TAESCH

> The following vignette is a repeat from "Short Stories" in *For all too soon*. No, I haven't run out of fresh things to write about. Hopefully, you may see my purpose when reading the anti-climax at the familiar end of the little story in retrospect. For those readers who have not read my first remembrance, bear with me for a short philosophical journey.

Lockhart

[Reprint with a new purpose]

In a sudden and surreal change, I slowly turn north away from the busy desert expressway. For a fleeting moment I am able to imagine the experience of one passing into heaven after leaving a long and turbulent life. The little side road – lined with tall trees – shades the way, not unlike a planted arbor of protective vines and lush moist green. Beyond the trees are endless expanses of irrigated land for the growing of man's sustenance. In the midst of *nirvana* is scattered a few old dwellings and a general store to serve the last remaining families who have worked this land for generations. Here, time has virtually stood still for at least a century.

If you travel in spring, butterflies upon thousands surround your vehicle as though a halo nearly clouding the view ahead, while painting the most colorful pastoral scene anyone could imagine. Agriculture and moisture have created a natural refuge and breeding ground for them. I stop for a cool soda at the general store and drink in the past and the peace. I often take drives into this area so as to view my vacant land beyond the little farm village. I believe that the drive through this lovely community is indeed the best part of my trip.

Escape with me now and imagine an old science-fiction movie – one about a remote country town where a strange craft from outer space has landed for a short visit. A lost traveler stumbles upon the village for gasoline and supplies, and discovers the residents to be in great fear of aliens who are slowly taking possession of their home. The driver speeds away, frantically trying to reach the next main city to tell his story. However, when he returns with journalists, the town is gone – nowhere in sight, and no one has ever heard of such a place.

Well, perhaps Richard's story is not quite as haunting, but after nearly twenty years of not visiting my nirvana, a friend and I decided to study maps and to seek out my land for a campout.

I must have passed the location of my familiar turn at least six times; it was not there and no sign was to be found. Taking a mere intuitive and desperate chance, I turned into a deserted road that vaguely resembled the general direction I sought. The pavement was full of potholes and appeared not traveled for decades - left in disrepair almost deliberately as though to discourage intruders. Nothing but barren desert and what appeared to be dried up fields could be seen.

Soon, empty shells of old dwellings and ruins of the familiar two-story general store came into view. A lone farmhouse was visible, fenced and still green as though a neutral island amidst the sea of dried cornfields and wasteland. What happened? Where? When, seem to be in my mind as I tried to convince my friend that what I described did, in fact, exist at one time.

After a moment of quiet thought he responded: "Richard, let's just drive a ways and see what's up ahead."

"Sure, if you want to, but ..."

Deeply disappointed, I was completely lost for any logical explanation. Suddenly there appeared to be the only possible answer to what happened here after the *aliens* came, raped the land, and destroyed nirvana.

Slowly, we passed the remains of fences that still had the dried skeletons of once thriving vines. Beyond them we could now see hundreds of acres of industrial solar panels, machinery, menacing barbed wire, and the stark reality of mass destruction of the secret garden – the once life-giving blood of families raised on the work that was no more. Crop growing and unimaginable beauty had been replaced with apparatus to power man's computers, video games, and insatiable thirst for energy. Was the land sold to the conglomerate, or were the inhabitants driven away from their home after generations of cultivating a perfect setting for the *new* corporate millennium?

As of this time, no evidence of Lockhart remains on some maps of the Golden State; but this lost traveler knows it did exist.... didn't it?

> Has virtual reality and instant access now become more important than butterflies? -- RT.

> Only when the last tree has died and the last river been poisoned and the last fish been caught will we realize we cannot eat money. -- Cree Indian proverb

California's broken promise

California is truly a great place, but its problems and taxes are as great as its history. I once learned that its name was from a fictional pagan warrior queen called *Califia* who ruled over a tribe of Arabic women in what is now Baja California.

The following reading for 2050 is based upon a real place and an ecological problem, but dramatized with a fictional, philosophical, and theoretical outcome. Look for key words that fill in the homework assignment blanks outlined in *The geography lesson* from Chapter 2.

The great desert Sea is only one of the many unique wonders of North America. Perhaps its current state in the throes of death is even a greater wonder, as its illness is a massive ecological mystery and debacle of the century. No, not the physical and scientific reasons for decline, but the political "turning of backs!" The loss of what was one of the greatest tourist attractions in the state is not only unthinkable, but completely unexplainable. To allow the last remaining wetland on the

Pacific Flyway - reaching from South America to the Arctic Circle - to become extinct may soon result in one of the worst ecological disasters in the last two centuries, with national and international ramifications.

Join me now as we imagine a troubled educator in the year 2050 attempting to make sense of a shameful piece of history to a class of high school students. The projected outcome, assumptions, and the characters are fictional.... we hope.

A classroom reading for the year 2050

[compare with Chapter II]:

"There was once an inland sea in North America; it was in a great desert that was once part of the ocean. Dried up for perhaps centuries, it reformed in 1906 due to an accidental diversion of the Colorado River, resulting in over 400 square miles of a new re-born sea. [Search: ***The Miracle in the Desert*** on Internet.]

"During the mid 1900s, it became known as the *California Riviera*. Boaters, fishermen, water sports enthusiasts, and celebrities swarmed to its shores. Warm temperatures all year round attracted people from everywhere. Investors and land promoters poured money into the area. Bird migrations from South America to the Arctic Circle came to depend upon this sea, creating national and international reasons to preserve it.

"Towards the end of the 1970s, flooding from agriculture runoff and an unexpected hurricane began the demise of the great *Salton Sea*. Resorts closed, hotels and business abandoned the area, and a naval base closed. Some new marinas and yacht clubs maximized the change, excavating new inlets at a higher water level. The flood waters then began to recede in the 1980s, leaving the new sea once again in ruins. Sea birds perished by the millions, massive fish die-offs were common, and many children died of respiratory complications. Toxic dust storms from exposed seabed still reach across the entire state and beyond."

"Ms. Jeffries," interrupts a young boy, "why does my map show Indian reservations near much of what once was the north-western shoreline?"

"Jimmy, as I understand it, these are tribes of Indian people still living in the valley. They depended on the sea for nearby agriculture, employment, and fishing to..." (Jimmy, once again, excitedly interrupts Ms. Jeffries):

"But this old map shows cities and towns all around the dry sea bed. If casinos and resorts are allowed on reservations, how could the sea just go away without being fixed? My book shows lots of failed solutions, but nothing mentions resorts that could have been put there!"

Ms. Jeffries hesitates, looking for an answer to give the puzzled child. "Well, Jimmy, perhaps other towns where gambling was OK were simply too close to compete with the potential growth, so they just let the sea go away."

"But that makes no sense to me."

VI

What if...

I suppose that some of my readers must know by now that Richard's autumn writings occasionally include fantasies of sorts, or perhaps "theories" is a better word. It does seem that many unresolved and puzzling situations lead to plays, movies, and books - some are fiction, some are not.

My remembrance, *For all too soon,* was based on real stories that I was a part of in some way. Where answers were not apparent, I asked: *Why is that?* Here, some are dramatized circumstances based on real things that I have known. However, I've expanded them with what I feel might be logical theories for unknown solutions. Chapter 6 is for fun, although mostly comprised of *What if ...* types of real situations. The events are imagined but quite possible. Some may even include rather disturbing outcomes.

SHORT STORIES - Points & Views #6

The Wearing (out?) of the Green - A letter to an editor

Dear Editor:

I would like to offer a special thanks to the Board for the wakeup call regarding expenses for our Journal. A donation or small subscription fee from those of us who prefer print or braille is a fine suggestion to help offset rising costs to our organization. I'd like to add my own friendly nudge for our members to consider helping with donations for journal costs. Clearly, our own MENVI [*Music Education Network for -The Visually Impaired*] would not have grown as much were it not for a certain amount of electronic delivery.

As to *helping the planet* by going online, it is my understanding that energy consumption in today's virtual computerized times is the highest in the history of the world and seems to be increasing exponentially. Not to mention that our landfills are hip deep in old computer waste. Could it be at all possible that we are adding to the problem by encouraging total virtual dependency? And as braillists, is that really what we want? Perhaps we might re-think equating *Green* to *online*, and simply ask for help with Journal costs.

Thank you for allowing a music person to speak out, as we all contribute a share of carbon footprints, *offline*. [Ed. RT]

The greenhouse

The annual science fair began with much enthusiasm along with technology-minded high school students eager to present their projects and theories. A new aspect to the event had been added: that of a debate to be carried out between two schools represented by students with opposing scientific theories. Winning entrants in the communications division were chosen to present their views on a paradigm shift from radio communication to earth- and satellite-based Internet providers. With overhead projection equipment, demonstration devices, and drawing boards in readiness, the race was on.

As the debate began, a rather cocky, young Jane Lopez opened her presentation with the preface: "Internet today has all but replaced over-the-air long distance dependency. In addition, it is far more reliable than ionosphere-bouncing of short radio waves around the earth."

Strategically avoiding a conflicting statement quite yet, Ira Jones responded with: "Miss Lopez, couldn't the massive and increasing gathering of live and dead satellites in earth's orbit alter incoming and outgoing functions of short-, or line-of-sight- radio waves passing near or through them?" Knowing Jane's knowledge of radio propagation was not her expertise, he continued: "Also, do you think that perhaps Internet satellites are not affected by this phenomenon? Can you kindly theorize on that for us?"

"That's not likely, as they do not appear to be affected by them as yet. Moreover, as radio dependency decreases or is eliminated, it would become irrelevant even if your theory is a factor."

"Would you then propose that we launch fiber-optic cables from earth to communicate with the International Space Station as a backup precaution?"

"Very funny!"

"Kindly explain then," persists Ira "if radio waves are affected by nearby metals as to wavelength resonance on earth, how can they not be affected by the metal materials in satellites? I am told that, at short distances from each other, they hurtle through space forming a near solid shell or *greenhouse* belt around us?" [Jones]

'I can't respond to that as my field of study is not in long distance. I only examine line-of-sight and cable installations for reliable and high speed data transfer. This afternoon, I will attempt to show superior reliability by means of improving technology, and how it works on behalf of consumers." [Lopez]

"Jane: What about the threat of sunspot disruptions interfering with satellite and Internet communication?"

"Certainly, that can interrupt it temporarily. But, Dr. Einstein," she adds sarcastically, "do they not interfere with radio propagation as well?"

"Jane, that's just my point! Sunspots are as crucial to good propagation as thermals are to a sailplane pilot, but dreaded as turbulence to commercial flights."

"So?"

"So, why would you advocate replacing ionosphere wave bounce with line-of- sight Internet without considering satellite interference or possible satellite failures, and not include protecting wave propagation as a necessary option?"

> As mentioned before, the current sunspot cycle is at an all time and worrisome low, whereas defunct satellite clutter is at an all time high and increasing. Long distance radio communication is also at an unprecedented low. Why is that?

Tales from the beyond

> The following story was written by Robert Walker, my treasured friend, mentor, and big brother in so many ways. He passed in 2016. This story was never published to my knowledge, other than a now out-of-print news journal. It has been edited somewhat for the non-radio hobby layperson. The message is quite ghostly, and a fine tale from the beyond.
>
> A **QSO** in radio terms is a conversational contact. This edited version of Robert's story is by permission of his daughter, Melanie Walker.

BEN'S LAST QSO

by

Robert Walker

I first met Ben over forty years ago. A young Engineer with a wife and two kids, I was struggling to make ends meet and operate Amateur Radio too. We were renting a small duplex in Lawndale, CA, and my equipment consisted of a home-built transmitter and an old *Hammarlund* Super-Pro receiver. He [Ben] was indeed an old-timer who grew up with spark transmission [very early transmitters]. I would sit spellbound as he told me tales of the good old days.

Ben helped my wife and I buy a new house in Bouquet Canyon. My wife said he was heaven-sent. My little girls, and my cat, adored him. A good man in every way--a good radiotelegraph operator he was as well.

But as time passed and we all got on with our lives, Ben retired, moved away, and I lost contact. Things didn't go well at home, and I was forced to sell my airplane, all radio equipment, and live on my boat. I couldn't afford anything else. Life does get tedious sometimes, but I survived, and I never forgot Ben.

Many years later with still modest but modern radio gear, I sat sipping some single malt scotch [whiskey] one winter evening and working a few East Coast stations on CW [continuous wave - radio telegraphy] for practice with my hand key. After signing off with a station in Baltimore, I paused for a break.

I savored the scotch; the cold wind moaned outside my window; the room was cozy and the receiver whispered softly as the *Bowmore* [brand of Scotch whiskey] warmed my insides. Resting my head on the desk for a minute, *dits* and *dahs* [dots and dashes] were still dancing in my brain.

Then, barely above the noise level in my receiver, I heard my call letters followed by Ben's "KB6... de [this is] K6.... Thinking I had misread the weak and fluttery signal, I answered. He returned: "is this Bob?"

"Yes, yes; your signal is very weak, but I copy!"

"Yes its Ben here. How are you, its' been a long time, how is family?"

"All gone Ben: divorce. Your signal is worse now, can you increase power?

"Yes" ...

"Sorry, Ben I can't copy at all now." The receiver hissed at me, and he was gone.

I sat up and sat back in semi-shock, gulped the rest of my drink and went to bed, somewhat disturbed to say the least.

About three or four years went by. I moved, things changed; the clock is relentless, but life goes on. I retired back in the hills with no [commercial] power or water, but still on the air.

One night at the low end of the 40 meter radio band, I tried again to contact Ben on about the same frequency as before, but nothing. After several tries, a super strong signal pinned my signal strength meter. After a few exchanges, for some reason he [the operator] asked if I knew Ben, as he must have recognized my call letters somehow from also knowing him.

"Did you know him well?" I asked.

"Yes, a neighbor and old friend; he loved the telegraphy mode. He passed away about 9 years ago!" [Long before Bob's contact (described above) with Ben.]

I signed off with a trembling hand and went QRT [quit transmission].

* * *

> Robert Walker was a corporate pilot, and a fine guitarist and vocalist in his own rite. He entertained around the desert community in small taverns with his dance combo. He recorded several original country songs, and loved the Indian folklore. The following short accounting is my own paraphrase - as best as I remember - of the message in his song about an American Indian man named Ezra Stone.

Ezra Stone

Bob's song describes Ezra Stone as of full blooded American Indian descent who lived on a small piece of land handed down through generations. He rode his horse daily, looking after his animals and modest crops for food.

One day two strangers rode in while prospecting, but out of sight of Ezra. They found gold on his land, but he was unaware. As I remember the story, the strangers shot and killed Ezra Stone then staked a claim to his land.

Time passed. One evening while looking up to a small rise above the property, they saw a dark ghostly shadow of a horseman looking quietly down at them. The headdress and feather was clearly visible - there Ezra sat on his pinto watching, watching, watching....

* * *

This review is about a play by an unknown (to me) television author for a popular science fiction program in the 1950s. Having been a sailplane pilot myself, I will never forget the brilliant and haunting storyline. I have only attempted to describe the epic here, as I have not been able to locate a source thus far.

The glider*

An oral description based on a science fiction television show, ca. 1950's

The story describes a glider pilot at a quiet airport about to take flight. His fiancé or perhaps it may have been his wife, stands by watching and waving as a tow plane pulls the aircraft into take-off, then fades in the distance. Releasing from the tow, the sailplane begins soaring on thermals to high and heavenly altitudes. Afternoon goes into evening, but no return or landing is in sight. Time passes....

Presumed lost, the pilot's wife returns to near the same area many years later on a picnic with a new friend. While visiting and lunching, she appears distracted by a far off sailplane circling, circling, circling, but does not seem to be setting up a pattern for landing. Her friend, feeling that she is experiencing a deep sentimental memory, tenderly offers encouraging conversation.

The plane, appearing exactly like the one her loved one left in many years before and never returned, begins to circle closer, and closer, now seeming to begin a landing approach. By now she is standing and completely absorbed in the aircraft. Her friend watches her intensely and seems quite worried about her behavior.

Finally the plane lands in whisper quiet very far down the runway area, which appears in my memory as quite deserted at this time. After landing, no one opens the canopy, and no one steps out! The plane sits in this frozen state for what seems to be a very long time. The girl, slowly and hesitatingly, begins to walk towards the ghostly sight, but her friend stops her and offers to approach the craft alone first; she agrees.

Carefully approaching from behind the cockpit, he sees the outline of a helmet and clearly that of a pilot's frame. As he walks around to see who it is, the grisly view of a skeleton grins and stares forward from beneath the helmet.

> *As said, the story was so stirring that I couldn't help but to offer my own impression of its content. In theory, pending just the right thermal activity, a sailplane could, in fact, remain in flight indefinitely. It can also be very difficult for the pilot to descend if nature maintains strong lift indefinitely as well. Such is not likely to happen in reality, but suppose that this tale from beyond did become reality for this pilot - this time....

SUMMER'S MEMORY

RICHARD E. TAESCH

Suppose this tale from beyond became a reality for this pilot
- this time

VII

Reflections from the bandstands

Writing about the past as in a remembrance has its advantages, as time and progression of one's life is a great aid in a natural story development. But I must say that the freedom of random choice of events as in a sequel, other than chapter groupings, has its own reward. Thoughts are often known to surface at the most unusual times. To not have to rewrite past chapters for insertions, one can invent a literary journey as the work moves along. In VII, I will be reaching back into more musical moments working in the performance arena. As seen in *For all too soon*, humorous and intriguing stories that only commercial musicians are likely to experience seem to be quite abundant.

VIGNETTES

Richard was invited to work as a sideman for a performer that he met while teaching commercial and jazz guitar classes at L.A. City College in the eighties. Bill was a student in my class there. Later, he hired me to back him with his combo for a top forty gig at an exclusive upstairs Hollywood night club. His show consisted of arranged charts to be read so as to frame a celebrity type of performance in rehearsed style. The players had never seen the music before downbeat at 10pm.

For background atmosphere, a very fine *Nordstrom's* - kind of house pianist of advancing years filled the room with music for cocktail hours and between featured shows. He would take requests, and seemingly knew all the standards that might be asked for. The club appeared to be his territory, as he most likely entertained some of the same guests there several nights of the week.

As the show was in progress, the gentleman mentioned above hobbled up to the bandstand and quietly began to lean towards me as if to speak. I thought it strange, as he could see me concentrating on the chart, and should have known better than to vie for my attention. In a kind of European-sounding accent, he asked if I could play a particular tune - a rather strange request considering the circumstances. Moreover, a pro would usually not behave this way at that time.

I responded to him: "I don't think I know that tune, but will check with the others as soon as we finish this set." [Hint, hint.]

He responded: "Well, son, you must not be a very good musician, now are you?"

I nodded and continued to read and play while trying to ignore him. He then insisted "You are not a good musician then; are you?" in a demanding tone.

I glanced over to him while continuing and said: "Of course not, sir; that should be obvious to a *good* musician like yourself."

Somewhat shocked by that, he frowned and went back to sit near his piano, grumbling, "Wise ass!"

He behaved as though a *has-been* comedian who picks a straight-man from the audience to heckle. Why he picked me, I know not. Perhaps he was put off by my large natural hairdo, or maybe the solid body guitar was not the Guy Lombardo- type of look. Something sent a bug up his you know where, there was no mistake about that.

A bit later, a band break was in order. I summoned our bass player to confer with while I bought him a beer. "Jim, did you see that old fart and the harassing he laid on me?"

"I sure did. What was the problem?"

"Not sure! But I've got a favor to ask, and I'll buy you a beer on each break if you'll pull it off for me."

"Like?"

"Well, when he's back at the piano looking like Van Cliburn in 2084, go up and ask him if he can play a request for you. Hold a five spot in your hand which I'll give you. When it's obvious he doesn't know the tune, grab the five out of the tip jar and boogie. Be sure some other customers are around."

"Got it; can't wait."

While *Liberace* was wound up in one of his syrupy hand-to-hand arpeggios, Jim asked: "Sir, do you know 'Spain' by Chick Corea?"

"By who? Never heard of the guy."

"Why sir; I guess that you must not be a very good musician."

He grumbled, looked up at Jim, then turned and glared over at me laughing my butt off. He then winked as though OK, you win (you think)! He smiled, stopped his tune cold then began to play a Thelonious Monk tune like a jazz pro. Touché!

And, the winner is....

One social service club would put on wonderful parties and events every year, and would always hire Jay Conner's band to play for dancing. I had worked for Jay many years. We were usually encouraged to leave our tuxes at home and wear casual garb to fit in with the less formal festivities on Halloween.

This particular year, the trumpet player decided to wear a kind of jump suit which, I must admit, appeared not unlike a worker's overalls. Jay was not on the gig that year and had appointed one of us to be interim leader in his stead. The following week he received a call from the club's president complaining about the sloppy appearance of one band member, namely the trumpet player.

The year went by, Halloween rolled around, and the club once again contracted Jay's band. When Jay called each of us to set the date of the dance, he asked for us to wear our tuxedos this year as he had a complaint the year before. Each of us tried to convince him of the fact that a tux might not fly on a Halloween gig. He insisted in typical boss-like tone: "it's my band, so do as I ask."

The ghostly evening came and we all showed up dressed as requested. Every one of the guests was, of course, decked out in very creative costumes while the festivities commenced. As the night progressed, the costume judging contest was about to get underway as expected.

Disguised guests paraded their frames one by one on the stage to be judged for the winning costume. The band sat nearby waiting to provide the winner's fanfare.

"And ..., the winner is: The orchestra - with the best costumes as *undertakers!"*

Jay cringed, frowned in a rather pissed manner, while the band grinned at him as if: told ya' so, Jay!

There goes the bride

When the band is invited to partake in the catered buffet at weddings, it is generally protocol and etiquette to wait until a go-ahead is given by the band leader. In most cases he has been given instructions. Once the bride, groom, and the bridal party have gone through the line, guests follow and the band joins at that point on a music break. Somehow, Howard the pianist must've missed that one, or perhaps this was his first wedding (fat chance of that).

Our wedding gig that week was at a fine upscale country club with a mouth-watering buffet waiting in anticipation of the formalities. About an hour into the festivities, the band took a break while dancers and guests sat down to prepare for the food serving to get under way. The long awaited announcement came. From across the banquet room, bride, groom, and guests one-by-one, began a slow but graceful procession toward the buffet table.

Howard, with no apparent awareness of anyone, stood and began his somewhat hasty assault on the food. He grabbed his plate and utensils from the stack, then stepped to the head of the line while the bride and groom quietly stepped back. They appeared not unlike an adult cat giving way to a rude kitten gobbling fast and furious before his or her siblings. Of course, all are staring at him as if: 'what's with this dude?'

He then returned to the table that his band mates had moved away from so as not to appear associated with him. Plate piled higher than a Dagwood sandwich, he plopped himself down while we casually pretended to not be connected in any way.

Sometimes my memory falters a bit, but I do think that one of the other players just happened to have his union - *anti-spy* - disguise wig in his instrument case. As I remember, leader Jay made Howard wear that wig for the rest of the gig. I can't help but to wonder if he even asked why.

Least, but not last*

Well, if there was one thing that our *all-knowing* band leader learned late, was to never play a Jewish folk dance in place of a tarantella at an Italian wedding.

Jay liked to appear somewhat in control of decisions that he required the band to follow. Having run out of Italian dances to play for the very folk-dance-loving guests, he commanded us to play a Jewish horah. This, even after the best man insisted on another tarantella. We rolled our eyes as the tune commenced, while up walked a very tall, angry, and somewhat gangster-looking well dressed fellow.

Now most groups, no matter the nationality, usually welcome all kinds of ethnic music for folk dancing, but apparently not to be this time. When Jay stepped up to announce another tune, the fellow confronted him. Towering over him he growled: "Don't you ever, ever play a horah at an Italian wedding." He looked down at Jay, even though Jay was near six feet tall. He bent over and went nose to nose with him like an angry parent to a kid who had misbehaved.

Now Jay was a near-retired policeman who sometimes still carried his badge. The band held its giggles while this fellow - unaware of the situation - was just about to tear him a new smile. The sight of our gracious leader looking up to this guy while repeating "yes sir," was a work of art to behold, indeed. It would have been even more entertaining if the fellow had added the gesture of putting one hand into his coat while he intimidated Jay. Moreover, what if he was also a cop? How much better the entertainment that afternoon could have been, no one will ever know.

More gig stories to come later....

VIII

As you believe

Traditionally, teachers often learn from their teachers and mentors. However, the greatest gift that any educator can pass on is how he or she has learned from students. Such is generally based upon a continuing self-analysis of collective experience.

For me, the precious lessons of my past were always a kind of subconscious compilation, guiding and watching as I went along day to day. I made mistakes and tried to learn from them, but never lost view of those who came before. Therefore, my personal philosophy for music teaching here is not meant as instructional. It is just a simple sharing of what worked for me. What I learned mostly, was to take serious notice of those little "voices" reaching out from within. As with many of us, when I did not, I was always sorry.

Similarly, take great care when you modify such instincts based upon doubts coming from *without*, as perhaps it might be best to get a second opinion first (your own). If one cannot trust those instincts, perhaps teaching is not for him or her.

There are music teachers who do not accept adult learners. But I often wonder just how many of them really know why. Some reasons that I have gathered from some of them are that adults:

1. don't practice

2. don't have time to prepare adequately
3. are far too critical of themselves
4. always quit after a short time
5. debate results and approaches too much, too soon
6. have too many conflicts: family, job, etc.

Many or all of the above may be true, but I believe that there is one simple and more comprehensive reason.

One of the expectations of becoming an adult is that of acquiring reasonably good judgment. That is, the ability to assess oneself in mature decision making in general. However, this *maturity* can often work against us in learning situations where we are not yet qualified to apply it. For example, when a teacher compliments as to a well prepared lesson piece, an adult student may doubt based upon what he or she perceives what the result *should* be. We are often unaware that we are not yet qualified to accurately assess that step. We may simply have inadequate basis to compare musical development. Otherwise, one would not be seeking a teacher, or depending upon his or her experience to help us improve. As pointed out in *For all too soon*, even Richard - already teaching - expressed to his teacher that he was worried about how he played a particular piece. His piano teacher, Charles Lewis, then expressed: *now, now, stop worrying; let me do the worrying, that's what you pay me for. If I think you need to worry, I'll be the first to tell you!*

Outtakes

It was quite early in my then student teaching appointment when I was commissioned to substitute two weeks for another teacher. This was a gentleman who was years ahead of me in professional experience and guitar methodology. The young student came into my studio and was quite fine with the temporary changing of the guard. I enjoyed the lesson, but was dazzled by his advanced level. The boy was already playing full solo arrangements by George Van Epps, a long time icon in our field.

When the teacher returned, I decided to make a phone call to him. I asked his secret of how he made such progress, and on such complex and technical material. I also inquired as to where I could acquire that publication. Almost instantly, he read my mind and evaluated my "time in the field." He then responded - not directly to my question, but with such wisdom that I was speechless: *Richard, when you teach, never, never do too much for your student.*

Yes, that was his answer! But perhaps some twenty years later it came to me what he meant. The man not only answered my question, but knowing the typical mistakes that he probably made along with others like me, did more for my professional growth than any class or book learning could ever hope to. His meaning came quite clear: never explain more than needed; never spoon feed knowledge. All meaning, if you deprive your student of working out what you have taught beyond reason, he or she will fail. Thus once again, the quotation by a most interesting fellow, yet one that I have never met:

> The great teacher never strives to explain his vision. He simply invites you to stand beside him and see for yourself.
> --The Rev. R. Inman

* * *

Generations later, I was teaching studio, jazz, and commercial guitar classes at Los Angeles City College. All of the students in my classes were adults - some preparing for demo work, and others for jazz band classes at the college. Part of the program included jazz studies requiring some knowledge of music theory such as applied to complex chord construction, sight reading, and improvisation. The latter two were usually easy for this level of players, but the academic side was, well, let's say, "...

in one head and out the other," so to speak. Some of these fellows even played with celebrity bands and had dazzling technique, but theory, not so well. Books and books have been written on the subject, classes have been taken, and teachers have often given up. Guitarists do seem to resist the subject once the first few pages are gone through.

Many texts on theory require weeks of basics first. They usually apply time on harmonic analysis, including Bach's chorales. This generally comes before approaching simple chord construction that can be applied to the jazz idiom for guitarists' use. Now, not to negate the necessity of such texts, as I have written several myself. Many of the working players have been self-taught and just don't have the time or patience to wade through them so as to theoretically build a *C13 flat 5 flat 9* chord, etc.

Consequently, I developed a few simple steps to use that did not involve any memorization, just follow my outline as is. In the time span of one evening's class, I had all 25 students each reciting the construction of any extended and expanded jazz chord that I could quiz them on. Of course it was not instant recitation, but accurate it was, and lots of smiling faces were prevalent.

***

Improvisation for class or private jazz studies in the early stages usually reveals students struggling for years on their own trying to make music only using the five-note pentatonic or blues scale. Formal study usually leads to expanded knowledge of scales and modes, but has little effect on making mechanical note playing sound like one thinks it should sound. Having experimented with a method of handling this problem in classes, I was successful with private students as well.

A simple three-step procedure usually resulted in about five years of development in one thirty-minute session. Needless to say, the average music store plunker might now evolve into a kind of quasi-pro sound, guaranteed to elevate any aspiring player's dream in short order.

In classes, the feedback from others hearing the change would be instant smiles, wows, and joy. In a private lesson, a basic cassette recorder always sat at my teaching position. Simply speaking, the process is summarized thus:

1. I would ask the student to improvise for a few measures. I would back him or her with a repetitive chord progression while letting the recorder run. We would then stop; I would stop the recording without playing it back quite yet.
2. The next step was to explain the "question and answer" phrasing of melody ideas then play and record again.
3. The last step was to ask the player to sing or hum along with what he or she was improvising, acting as a kind of "mirror" of the sound.

We would then sit back and play all three recordings. The contrast between each step was dramatic! The student sat in disbelief while hearing lines that went from beginner, to musical, then onto years and years of musical growth! "Is that really me playing?" was often expressed. Of course, these were short excerpts, but opened doors and motivated the player in a way that would delight any music teacher over and over again.

*　*　*

Although I never chose to be a concert performer, *Classic** guitar occupied a very active place in my music teaching career from about 1975. It has been said that if one wants to expand his or her knowledge quickly - teach! Although having taught commercial and basic guitar since 1961, when I first began to take on classic guitar students, I began to feel that there was something seriously missing in the usual pedagogical approaches to the art.

Method after method, including continuing students from other teachers, began to reveal that most current approaches begin by rote. They are soon followed by note recognition on the staff, pointing to the strings and frets that produced them. Drills with two or three notes are assigned and continue until all six strings in first fret position are covered. If that was not enough to put your student to sleep, it surely would make a teacher's eyelids begin to quiver. Boring is an understatement, not to mention about as non-guitaristic as it gets.

I decided to temporarily circumvent guitar methods and to dissect methodology used in introductory theory classes at universities and community colleges. I then reached into my own experience with *Music 101*, and re-discovered that no matter what one's instrument or goal was, most approaches included simple keyboard harmony while advancing further.

The usual class - very early in the course - will generally require the student to learn basic keyboard root-position tonic, subdominant, and dominant (C, F, G) chord positions. Next we learn how to accompany simple melodies played by a tutor. This is meant to train the ear to know when to change a chord, thereby introducing the five-finger ground level geography of tonal music itself. This is not intended to teach the piano, but used as a graphic learning tool! Note reading and staff notation remain secondary at this juncture.

Now enters the guitar for scene II. I then began the habit of teaching simple chord accompaniment through basic chord shapes: strumming and familiar folk and pop tunes - NO note reading yet! Students were not required to know how to sing, but perhaps just to hum or recite lyrics. If they could put up with Richard's *cat-a-wailing*, all went well. Once a few chord shapes are under the fingers on a guitar, a student can more readily see how the individual notes are derived in harmony. He or she can then relate them to fingerboard geography.

If one delves further into history, even J.S. Bach who is said to have played the lute although not well, thought from chord structure upward in his writing. The *chord-first* concept is natural for a multi-string instrument. Bach's four-part chorales are often studied first by composition students, and so forth. These are fundamental to all music, and classic guitar is no exception. Perhaps one of the most impressive classic guitar players that I remember was my own teacher for a class at Long Beach University. He began as a folksong player and performer!

Beethoven is said to have stated that the guitar is like a miniature orchestra.

In the seventeenth century, one quote reads as: "So popular did the guitar become, that the English court scene was described as one of *universal strumming.*"**

One caveat: I would more than strongly advise explaining this approach to an adult student, particularly if he or she has come to you requesting specifically to learn the classic guitar. Otherwise, one may think that you are ignoring their desire and pushing pop music upon them. Ask me how I learned that! *Too soon auld; too late schmart.* With adult students, one can never be too cautious.

*The term **classical** guitar is thought by some as an unfortunate misnomer. "Classical" is a stylistic period in music history. **Classic** is often preferred, as it covers all periods for which the guitar is capable. **Spanish Guitar** is often used for books written or edited by greats such as Andres Segovia.*

**Quote taken from: The Baroque Guitar, by Frederick Noad - Page 95*

* * *

While quietly watching his lady friend softly strumming simple chord forms from her recent guitar lesson, Tony asks: "Marcy, I see a lot of my favorite jazz and blues players seeming to move all over the fingerboard, and really fast. How come I never see you trying to move your fingers out of those same basic positions?

'Well, honey, they do that because they keep looking and searching for that illusive *magical* note. Me, I've already found mine."

* * *

The little girl was quite bright and eager to learn. She was left-handed, which can be an advantage for fingering challenges presented

| 73 |

to young guitar beginners. The lesson interview with her parents commenced as follows:

"Sir, where would you suggest that we have her guitar re-strung for left hand playing?" demanded mom. "I am a pianist, and also left-handed."

"Mrs. ___, that won't be necessary, as she should begin as any right- or left-handed student would."

"Mr. T, forgive me, but I strongly disagree! What is your reason for that approach?"

"Well, consider that the greatest physical challenges for any beginner on a string instrument are in the left hand techniques. As such, a left-handed person may have a unique advantage as a beginning player."

Mom was clearly not impressed nor seemed to digest any reasoning. She was pre-disposed to her own *as you believe* convictions. I then tried one last presentation thus:

"Mrs. ___, you are a long time musician and apparently of an impressive background in your work as a keyboardist. May I ask a question?

"Of course!"

"According to your strong feelings on this subject, when you were beginning your own music as a child, surely your parents must have known to request that the piano be restrung for a left-handed player. That is with low notes on the right end of the keyboard, and high register on the left. Is that not true?"

* * *

The marketing of a pro music teacher often seems to me no more than a popularity contest. Slogans like: ... *taught for over... years, performed with...* [well-known celebrities], and brochures with smiling studio poses, etc. certainly are impressive and a fine indication of good business and self promotion. But as said before, "what about the students?"

Do indulge me to offer a rather risky opinion. Yes again, Richard's observations are his own; so do forgive the trespass should I offend the ambitious and successful entrepreneur just because *Mr. T* voluntarily chose to remain in the wings. Do read on.

Many respected and honored music teachers often seem to be those that I've either observed but not met, or friends and colleagues. All seem to have a track record of caring and living their musical lives to be the best they can be in the interest of those who have placed their trust in them. Mistakes, yes, but learning anew, always! Most of them seldom promote publicly nor spout credentials. And they are not generally found with full-page picture ads in music educators' journals with the caption: ... *now <u>accepting</u> students for fall*. Moreover, occasional recitals notwithstanding, such are uniquely humble and some often avoid the performance arena altogether.

Most never know that they are revered and held in such high esteem by some of us. I don't recall any one such treasured teacher who has not been the first to compliment other colleagues, speak highly of them, and always make the effort to take attention from themselves in favor of another.

IX

Highlights

If one were to write about all of the students who have made Richard look good, or friends that have made him feel good, this little book would end up being longer than *For all too soon!* But alas, a few special highlights should fill this chapter quite well.

I do find that music people, whether colleagues or students, often find very similar interests in common. For example, I met my friend from *Ben's Last QSO*, Robert Walker, when I was learning to fly sailplanes. He was hard to get to know, as he somewhat avoided people in general. Somehow he reminded me of my father. While observing him checking the vitals on an old WWII Cessna tow plane, I said hello and made some comment about the aircraft. He just said, never looking my way: "Yes, it takes a lot to keep the old war birds in the air."

We came and went but never really met, so I left it at that. One day while I was waiting to make a solo flight, he walked up to me while I was having lunch at a shaded picnic table. He asked if that was my car parked nearby. I said yes, and waited. "Well, I couldn't help but notice your license plate; are you a ham?" (Amateur Radio operator)

"Yes!" I responded. (My call letters serve as the license plate number, and are FCC issued.)

We soon began chatting; he was also a ham, a guitar player, played a few gigs around the desert, and liked a beer at the end of the day.

Over time we became life-long friends and spent much time together enjoying the hobbies that we loved.

During the good years at our five-acre campus, resident blind students came from many places to study intensively for two-week sessions. One young lady was attending Yale University, and was a trumpeter in the Yale orchestra. As such, she needed to concentrate on her braille music reading skills and computer music arts as well.

Kathleen was a hand full at best, and would object to most corrections as though an opportunity to quarrel. She was quite feisty to say the least, but somehow a lot of fun to know and work with. *Bright* is an understatement. Catching me in an error seemed to make her day.

While I was teaching her in the little *Sleeping Beauty* cottage where my office and braille production center was located, we had our daily disagreement, finished the lesson, and prepared to move to the next scheduled sessions of the day. As she got up to leave, the conversation continued as I mentioned some analogy of braille to the Morse code. She whirled around and growled: "Yeah? .... Well I teach the *bug* [semi-automatic telegraph key] to blind radio amateurs for the Library of Congress *Handi-Ham* program."

"Yikes! You've got to be kidding!" I responded.

First of all, young women hams are few. Even if they only hold an entrance level license, to be into the telegraphy part of the hobby is rare indeed, as it is no longer a requirement for any level of license. Moreover, she could handle the *Vibroplex*™ semi-automatic key well over thirty words per minute. No doubt she was probably faster than I was being rusty. She also had a higher class of radio license than I did! Guess who had the upper hand from that day to the end of her stay at the school?

* * *

While our Braille Music Division was operating at the large estate SCCM campus, we received a braille library donated by a retired blind pianist and educator. Prior to that, it had been kept at a major university. Sometime later, John contacted me regarding a planned trip to California. He wanted to include a stop at SCCM to see where his library was being housed. He routinely made the journey each year to play at a special recital. The program was hosted by his past adult student who would showcase himself and perform for friends. Such was a wealthy businessman who opened his impressive mansion yearly for the event, catered by a famous chef.

John came, toured our school, and was able to see his wonderful books resting in dignity within our braille library. He then invited me to the recital event and asked if I would bring a blind student to perform as well. He did indicate that his past student was a successful financier, and could be in a position to offer a grant to our program. He felt the effort might be beneficial to our school for the braille program. I selected one of my music braille students that I also coached in jazz studies, and who studied piano with my colleague and co-director.

The dinner, catered by *Wolfgang Puck*, was an outdoor affair under special tents. The food was perhaps the finest I have seen catered anywhere! My student, a young teen and gifted jazz pianist since about age nine, enjoyed his invitation to dine. He then prepared to perform following the feast.

After dinner, a small recital hall inside the majestic home began to collect an elite, well-dressed, and rather mature audience. The host and featured performer made some announcements then introduced the boy on the program. Before Charles's performance, *host* played a few standards intended to set a relaxed mood. Following the overture, young Charles - white cane and all, was led up to the Steinway. He took his place at the piano while host and onlookers prepared for a few pieces typical of a youngster at 15 years old.

The boy began with a medley of about six very hip jazz tunes with extended improvisations. Host appeared somewhat uneasy, well knowing that he was about to be upstaged and no way to stop it. Charles played with much humility, but as the true artist that he was. Before he was scheduled to finish, host steps up, generates an applause, and smiles with a condescending grin. He then leads Charles from the piano while members of the audience continue clapping and trying to reach out to him, touching his arms as he passes.

Host then stepped up to perform quite nicely, but not unlike one who has clearly stepped all over his proverbial proboscis. Incidentally, no attempt to offer grant funding ever came to be, and no further communication from *el businessman* or past teacher was ever heard.

* * *

After the closing of our failed La Canada campus, the SCCM relocated to a re-furbished building in the West Hills area of San Fernando Valley. One of my first visiting blind students was a young lady who was attending Stanford University. She was in the last stages of earning her Masters in music education and was required to complete some studies, namely music braille as applied to piano pedagogy.

As I anxiously awaited her arrival for a one-day intensive session, I stood watch for some kind of chartered transportation to appear so as to welcome her. Soon a sports car drove up and out stepped a young woman heading toward our school entrance. Not expecting a sighted person at that moment, I asked if there was anything that I could help her with.

"Hello," she said, while indicating that she was looking for Richard Taesch.

"I am he; may I ask your name?" I beckoned.

The last thing that I expected was a blind student driving up in an automobile for a full day session in braille! I just stood and starred.

"Oh, Richard: I'm so glad to meet you; and yes, you look shocked to see me driving."

"Uh, well, yes, kind of ... uh,"

It turned out to be a first for me! She explained that it was a very rare vision loss that caused her to lose the center of vision when she focused on print to read. She had read braille since a child, and studied at the Louis Braille Center in Paris before coming to the United States. A *highlight* it was, indeed!

* * *

Perhaps one of the most inspiring VI teaching experiences for me was that of a young lady named Andrea. She came to us as a young teen, and stayed in the program until near age 23. Andrea had studied piano for some time before coming to SCCM, and achieved rather advanced levels using print music. Chopin, Bach, and more contemporary composers were quite well under her fingers.

Her vision began to fail during those years. With an uncertain road ahead, her school recommended that she consider our program. Once she realized that braille would be her best option in preference to large print, a rather bleak outlook began to open new doors for her.

Andrea studied music braille for a year or two with me, and concurrent piano with my colleague, Grant. Her vision was still possible, but difficult. However, when given an equal choice to read large print vs. music braille, her preference was always braille! Imagine learning a Chopin etude in print then becoming equally comfortable with braille. In my own experience, this was perhaps the first student that I had worked with that was able to do that. Many blind-from-birth youngsters often learn to read music braille as well as a print reader reads print. But to reach the level that Andrea did, then switch as a teen while taking it in stride as "no big deal," was a first.

Outtake:

One day Andrea came into class sporting a very short, but attractive new hairstyle. Her beautiful long hair was stunning, and why she made the choice to have it cut was a shock to most of us at the school.

She made no effort to discuss it, and tended to change the subject. She seemed to express no regret whatsoever. It later came out through typical gossip that she had chosen to donate her hair to a program for children with cancer, whereby young girls had lost their hair due to chemotherapy.

X

The cynics

It seems that as one grows older, the easier it becomes to express one's inner - often non-politically correct - views. Speaking only from Richard's *point and view*, how one is observed by others gradually becomes subordinate to a maturing self image. That is to say, being less politically correct at times no longer threatens one's alter ego, nor the youthful need to protect it. It is what it is, and we become increasingly more comfortable with it.

Now in my fall season, make no mistake in that Richard would never have been quite as candid when writing *For all too soon*. At times now, he sinfully indulges himself in the *luxury of being cynical*!

If you are at all a curious observer of trends and attitudes, as said in my fall introduction, when writing your own story as I have here, you may be writing for all of us at one time or another. With John Steinbeck I am not to be compared, but he wrote it as he saw it, and a role model he seems to be for many authors.

Over time, Richard became a dedicated observer, resulting in a cautious critic of evolving trends in human behavior. Having been born and raised in South Cal, clearly fostered (and heightened) many rather unsettling hypotheses

The late director and founder of Southern California Conservatory of Music (SCCM), was someone that you did not always like. But deep down you always loved and respected her. At her memorial service, I was privileged to give a short tribute to her. With respect to our years as faculty at SCCM under her direction, I made the comment that her faith in what she saw for her school gave me and my co-director the "luxury of being cynical." Meaning that, in many discouraging situations throughout our troubled years, her faith was what pulled us through. Were it not for that, Grant, my co-director and I would not have been able to depend upon humor to keep us believing in the mission that we were all a part of. One definition of that humor can be summed up as: A pessimist is: *an optimist with experience.*

That being cautiously said, I would like to share a tongue-in-cheek dictionary for the dedicated pessimist who still retains his or her mission as an optimist.

THE CYNIC'S DICTIONARY OF COMMON TERMS

app a trendy name for a computer program devised to intimidate old folks

axiom (example of) the outside diameter of the bath tissue roll remains constant while the inside diameter seems to increase exponentially with the price

business ethic a once noble practice applied to fair and necessary exchange; now being redefined by some, whereby one takes as much as can while giving back as little as possible or nothing at all

class action collective butt-kicking

consumer self-protection clause (e.g.) we've got 'em right where they want us

cynic a self motivated seeker of truth and fact, outwardly critical of promotional interests

dear valued resident a quasi form letter salutation often used by management so as to endear a renter, while deferring the actual intent of the document

due to a phrase generally preceding fee hikes or increases in cost

economy model compared to what?

free offer an opportunity for you to spend money

go green save paper, send e-money

go paperless promote e-waste / fight recycling

inflation the process of increasing corporate profits while decreasing product quantity and quality - when we want more, you get less

internet server a computerized telephone switchboard

landfill 1. a place for depositing old computers and used shipments from Amazon 2. a covert real estate investment for future condominiums

late fee a profitable business solution whereby, when you can't afford to pay on time, the fee increases so as to make it harder to meet, thereby a higher profit

marketing how to make a commodity or service appear to be more than it is

mental indigestion 1. a temporary condition that occurs when one first opens the latest magazine issue for retirees 2. an automated response caused by flamboyant eye-straining graphics that leap into one's face and beckon: *do this, buy that, live longer, sex at 80,* etc. - all jammed into a few pages of the newest *ACG* periodical (American Coalition of Geezers) .

mobile home park a place where one puts a home on someone else's property so as to increase the landowners' profits, while proportionally decreasing home value as well as the home owner's bank account

97/3 a virtual facsimile for ground beef soaked in a reddish-colored brine solution, tasting not unlike a shredded tax return. It is then shrink-wrapped and labeled "Extra Lean"

.99 cents a deceptive label that pertains only to the last two figures of any price, often preceded or followed by the word "only"

open immediately do not open; go directly to trash

pessimist an optimist with experience

petition enclosed a request for donation is enclosed

politician a public servant empowered by the people to take money from them

promotional offer don't bother to open

sent from Joe's iPhone a trendy status symbol that appears with Joe's name

save a tree upgrade now - send money

speaker phone a barrel within which folks talk on a telephone. A cover is often placed over the barrel so as to create an unintelligible garbled echo

technology 1. a science that often outpaces its purpose 2. a science often valued beyond, or in preference to, its benefits

truth a pre-millennium fact that has become obsolete in the virtual world (such often requires a password)

survey enclosed see "petition enclosed"

urgent 1. same as "open immediately" 2. trash before opening

virtual 1. fake 2. nothing is real

virtual reality strawberry fields

wireless the distance to the nearest cell tower

zero interest wanna' bet?

XI

Careers

I've had the honor of knowing many dear people who have had the most amazing careers. As with others, most of their accomplishments go unnoticed in the later years, or completely forgotten even after they have passed. While autumn surrounds me, their memory and stature seems to occupy my thoughts more often than when they were mere colleagues or just special friends with family and interests in common. Perhaps this is a good thing, as true living friends usually do not regard each other as special because of their status or titles.

In this chapter, I would like to offer several rather short vignettes as examples of such people and what or who they were outside of our friendship. Sadly, most are now passed. Moreover, their significant roles have faded within the mainstream of daily life that once surrounded them. These little accountings are in their honor: who they were as I saw them, and why their significance will never fade from my memoires. The last is about every hiker's friend, one we have most likely never met.

Their names have not been changed out of respect for their memory. All were very highly regarded while they were living.

VIGNETTES

Fred was a musician that I met on a country club gig in Montebello. Never having met before, we shook hands, introduced ourselves, and proceeded to play dance music for a private party attempting to sound as if we had rehearsed for it. Generally, musicians are admonished by their bandleaders to never shake hands on the bandstand. As such, patrons might assume that you had never played together before. (They are often quite right.)

I was fairly new at live performing where there were no formal arrangements, only the playing of tunes that one was "supposed to know" as a black suit and tie society musician. I apologized to Fred, as I was treading water pretty much throughout the whole evening. His kindness, complimentary and non-condescending attitude left a permanent impression on me, and a life-long bond was formed.

As time went on, Fred and I played many engagements together. Later as a well-seasoned "gigster," I took my place along with the rest of the *bowtie set*. Soon we became social friends - backpacking, day hiking, and trips to Disneyland with him and our wives were among frequent activities.

Besides being a fine alto sax player and flautist, Fred's day job consisted of being a math and physics teacher at Grant High School. He also gave much volunteer time to helping youngsters study for the SAT tests on Saturdays. He formed a school backpacking club, often bringing one or two students along on his family backpacks each summer.

Fred was loved by all of his flock, so much so that the *Valley Magazine* (April, 1997) published a full story with photos of him and his students in the classroom. His demeanor somewhat reminded me of the teacher portrayed in the true story movie, *Stand and Deliver*. Mr. C (Fred) was warm, determined, and a friend to all of those under his tutelage, always putting everyone else's needs before his own.

One year he was nominated for the prestigious *American Teacher Award*. A major event was held in Los Angeles. Friends, colleagues, family, and students turned out to support and honor him. Another teacher was just ahead of Fred for the award, but to be nominated and loved in such a way was quite sufficient for him.

Having taught for Los Angeles Unified School District (LAUSD) over 42 years, an administrator informed Fred that he would make more money retired than teaching. He retired and continued teaching part-time until another administrator decided that he was low-man on the totem pole and let him go. He then began a series of part-time teaching positions, and finally began to teach a couple of physics classes at Pierce Jr. College. Failing eyesight then caused him to give up teaching altogether.

His diminished eyesight led to a bad fall which left him crippled. Eventually, he transitioned to board and care facilities then later to home health care. Fred passed quietly one night in his sleep soon after his family had met for dinner in the dining room of the house.

His memorial was held at the church where he had served as an elder, sang in the choir, and played both flute and sax for services. Folks came from everywhere to honor this giant of a man who changed the lives of young people and made everyone he met feel important!*

*Fred's story here is edited and included by permission of his wife, Karen.

* * *

Ruth was a neighbor at the time I first moved into the mobile home community that I called 34th Street in *For all too soon*. She was elderly but quite trim - tall and well preserved in a model way. She kept to herself tending her little flower gardens around a small and modest mobile home. Most neighbors did not know much about Ruth and assumed that she was without much family, as no one was ever seen visiting.

Through occasional chats with our park manager, the conversations often revealed humorous gossip pertaining to different residents. One afternoon an incredible story became the discussion de jour.

In the early days following the opening of the mobile home park, wilderness and wildlife were a common part of the sparsely populated community. This particular afternoon, Ruth quietly meandered down to place her refuse in the community dumpster. She opened the lid, began to lift the bag of trash into the container, and out jumped a full-grown mountain lion scavenging for food. Now, it's hard to say just which one of the two was startled the most! Ruth dropped the bag, ran *tush-n'-elbows* as fast as she could in one direction! The big kitty - eyes wide with terror - ran in the opposite direction, both screeching like two sopranos in different keys.

Time went by, and Ruth was not seen around her home for quite a few weeks. It finally came to be that she had suffered a stroke and was now in a nursing home. Ruth passed penniless, alone, and with no advanced directives. Her home and belongings went to probate and the memory of her faded. It turned out, unknown to any of us, that in her youth she and her husband had been famous aerial trapeze artists in their home country of Holland.

* * *

At the time I joined the Music Teachers' Association of California (MTAC) in 1970, I was perhaps one of the youngest members of my branch at about thirty years old. Many of the branch members were elderly professionals that, after retiring from performing, taught music privately.

Helen was a new member of our branch with a very *old world* and dignified appearance. Her silver hair tied in a bun and very straight posture raised visions of opera houses, silent movies, unquestioned etiquette, and great white mansions with music parlors and chamber recitals. Earlier in her life, Helen was a commercial pianist, organist, accompanist, and lecturer.

As time passed, she began finding herself alone and with very few students. Helen clearly missed the good years with high society engagements and the active lives of folks with whom she had worked. One day she joined a senior singles group, met an elderly gentleman, and married. James always came along with Helen to the music teachers' events and recitals. They were a model couple and might have been any one's great grandparents, always dressed perfectly with James in suit and tie.

Still confident that she had the pianistic technique to play a home recital, Helen planned a special treat at her home for her MTAC colleagues from our branch. This was a special program of fine repertoire, and refreshments served in a teahouse manner - quite typical of an eighteenth century parlor gathering. It was a lovely affair, but years away from the concert stage, aging joints, and waning technique took its toll on her and what she had hoped her performance should have been. I believe that, like Richard's last gig, Helen left the concert stage for good.

Not more than one year after their wedding, James fell ill and passed. Helen was once again alone but remained in very good spirits. My own marriage had just ended, and she would often talk with me on the phone offering motherly comfort and tips on making balanced meals as a new divorcee. Never learning to cook myself, any information beyond can openers was quite welcome.

Soon thereafter, she stopped coming to meetings and kept to herself. My last phone visit with her was when she had moved to an assisted living home. I had made plans to visit with her there but, *for all too soon*, Helen was no longer with us.

Postlude

Before she passed, I was honored to introduce a friend to Helen for an interview. He was in process of writing his doctoral dissertation. The work would later become a historical treatise published by Johns Hopkins University Press. The book included an article about the end of silent pictures and the beginning of sound, thus ending the era of the pit musician and organ accompanists in the early movie houses. It was then I learned that my little silver-haired colleague had once been the highest paid and only woman theater organist in the Chicago area! She had been so respected, that her presence was required when the grand pipe organ was being tuned as her standards were exacting. [Search: ***Stage to Studio*** - *James P. Kraft* - Hopkins Press]

***

Among many things, naturalist John Muir was also known to be the founder of what is known today as the *Sierra Club*. Anyone who has done backpacking, extensive day hiking, or even simply being involved in nature for self therapy, will know about him. A large section of Pacific Crest Trail (PCT) in the California Sierra Nevada mountain range is named, the *John Muir Trail*.

Like many of us, some of our most treasured friends can be philosophically diametric to our own beliefs with little or no negative impact on our friendship. As careers go, one such friend of Muir, Gordon Pinchot, was the first director of forestry in the U.S. John was deeply committed to the belief that nature should be carefully protected and conserved for the benefit of those to come. He felt that man's needs should not come first so as to promote squandering and wasteful consumption of natural resources. Gordon, on the other hand, appeared to believe that nature should be freely consumed and only exists for that of man's benefit.

As I understand the story, their differences were generally not disruptive, other than perhaps a heated debate now and then; not unlike two folks discussing different political beliefs. Both may be passionate in their feelings, but a joke or two now and then might go a long way to cushion the impact. And so it seemed to be with John and Gordon until a heated conflict in 1913 over an impending plan to dam a river that affected American tribal lands. The plan would create the man-made *Hetch Hetchy* Reservoir in northern Yosemite National Park, thereby destroying a natural habitat and the course of history as well. As outcomes go, Gordon's preference won.

Apparently having taken ill, John Muir died broken-hearted knowing that the project was approved.*

RICHARD E. TAESCH

" *Climb the mountains and get their good tidings. Nature's peace will flow into you as sunshine flows into trees.*
-- John Muir "

Search: **Restore Hetch Hetchy** *on Internet*

* * *

Students honor Mr. C - Fred

XII

Strangers

There are times in all of our lives when we meet strangers who later may even become some of our most treasured friends. While searching through my mental library looking for a good segue from *Careers,* my thoughts suddenly wandered into a thread of strangers that I met through the many miles of hiked trails and solitary meanderings. These are not strangers that necessarily became friends. They are those who created such a warm and special place in my memory, that I seem to have somewhat kept them to myself. Perhaps I was feeling either protective of those moments, or simply setting them aside as of surely no interest to others. All share a common place of never having been seen again - "willow the wisps" of sorts, lost in private places. Such is a world often belonging to musicians, songwriters, and poets who are willing to share them through creative ways as fantasies. Believe them or not, and if not, nothing is lost.

Come with me now to that special world of very short, but meaningful experiences. No dramatizing or journalistic expansion has been added. If by chance one of the characters described in this little collection happens to read it one day, do know that our meetings were not lost in time! The presentation is random, but in the order that they came to mind as literary sketches.

Richard loved hiking out of the Tapia Canyon trailhead on Malibu Canyon Road in the early eighties. He would hike from the parking area, climb the dirt trails to the crest of the mountains overlooking the ocean, then descend downwards to Pacific Coast Highway (PCH) just north of Pepperdine University - a jaunt of about nine miles. He would lunch at *Malibu Seafood* restaurant, then cross the famed U.S Highway 1 to settle for a nap on the sands of Corral Beach before sunset.

This particular day just happened to be the Fourth of July holiday. I was somewhat surprised to see so many Mexican families camping on the beach until I realized what day it was. "Drat! I was hoping to be somewhat alone." No matter where I walked with my daypack on, there was another family tending a little bonfire, chatting, singing in Spanish, and sharing the fun.

"Oh well, I'll just wander till I find a place to sit, sprawl, and nap." Not to be; each family that I would pass stopped me and wanted to have me share their meal and sit with them. Now, what they were barbequing certainly smelled tempting. However, I politely declined as my mind was set on going back to *Malibu Seafood* for fish and chips before the night trek back to my car.

It soon dawned on me after a short interpretive conversation in Spanish, that they viewed me as a homeless fellow packing along the beach. After all, I must have stood out among the gathering as a sweaty, dusty, and very weary traveler as opposed to a day hiker with a car parked nine miles away. Imagine a beach full of wonderful amigos, all wanting to offer friendship. Clearly, there were no strangers amongst any of us that day.

* * *

A bit later that season, I mounted the same hike just following the Labor Day weekend. This time I was quite aware of the past holiday and hoping that the beach would probably be somewhat deserted towards the late day when I would arrive. It was, and after settling on the sand for a while, the thought of Malibu Seafood fish and chips was again tugging at my appetite.

As I strolled a ways down the beach, I noticed a lone transient under the bridge that goes under PCH from Corral creek. He said hello and waved warmly. I acknowledged, and couldn't help but feel one of those: "... there but for you ..." moments. I walked towards him and said "are you OK?"

"Oh yes; just getting settled down for the night."

I replied: "I have some trail mix in my pack, could I interest you in a bag?"

"I sure would like a little something, as it's been a lot of walking today; kinda' wore out."

I took out the pack of trail mix and handed it to him, turned, and began to leave him to his privacy. As I walked away, all fear and caution left. I turned around and asked: "Hey man; I'm going over to the seafood place for a fish dinner to sit on the sand and enjoy. Would you like for me to bring you one before I begin my hike back over the crest?"

Realizing that I was not a *bro* homeless too, he smiled and said: "Man, I'd truly like that! Are you sure that's OK? I have a dollar or two, if you want ..."

"No way! I'd like to do that. Be back in a short while."

I left, hiked back across the busy highway and returned. We sat together for a while and silently enjoyed the usual Malibu, very *one-of-a-kind,* fine meal. We then bid goodbye as I started my nine mile hike back in the dark to whence the day had begun.

* * *

Another routine hike in the San Gabriel Mountains brought a very chance meeting with a fellow who often frequented the Strawberry Peak trail. I was heading south on the trail planning a loop trip back via Pacific Crest Trail, when I passed a hiker attempting to settle down for the night in a small trail camp. We waved, chatted a moment or two, and I was on my way.

Later, I decided to return the same way instead of the loop plan. Now dark, I spotted the fellow in fire lit shadows warming himself by his campfire while drinking a can of beer. As I passed in the dark hoping to not alarm him, he called out a friendly hello and asked if I wanted to stop for a while and join him for a beer. He was apparently well stocked on a supply of "suds," and needless to say, I accepted the invitation. There we were in the middle of the forest, chatting and laughing as though long time friends, trading stories of the trails, sipping, and enjoying the warm fire. It was a simple story, no intrigue out of the usual - nothing special as most folks might view it; just another chance meeting. As a warm rain began to fall, I was once again on my way. We have never crossed trails since.

* * *

Coming home late one night within the first few years of moving to my new country home, a tire went flat no more than a mile from my destination. I was on a narrow upgrade before the crest, and at that time there were few road lights; it was pitch dark with no moon and no passing traffic. Having pulled off of the road, I attempted to lift the right rear end of the 4K LB car that I was driving with a wobbly bumper jack so as to change the tire.

Well, due to the incline, I couldn't quite clear the ground to remove it. So there I sat - now what? There was no cell phone to call Triple A, and no one in sight. Suddenly headlights appeared behind me and slowly came to a stop behind the old Pontiac. A man - very slowly - stepped out, cautiously trying to assess the situation in the very dark night. As he came closer, I was now convinced that, in the darkness, he was my new neighbor. I said: "Richard!" (We shared names.) "Wow, am I glad to see you!" He seemed puzzled, as though not understanding, but offered:

"Can I do something to help?"

All must have seemed safe, so he kindly offered to temporarily inflate the tire so as for me to make it home. This seemed doable, as I was quite close to home in the deserted canyon. There we chatted while a small battery-operated pump worked to bring the tire up to pressure for the short run to safety. As the conversation went to things that should be familiar to two neighbors, he suddenly stopped as though confused.

"Look, Mister, I don't know you, and we've never met before!" There seemed to be some new apprehension in his voice, as I realized I had made an error to mistake him for someone else in the dark. Embarrassed, is an understatement!

"Oh my god, I'm so sorry! I've mistaken you for my neighbor, as we haven't been neighbors for very long." I'm sure he must have been thinking - 'nut case - likely story, wonder if he'll rob me?'

All was soon resolved, and I thanked him profusely. He said to me while heading back to his car: "You're most welcome! Maybe you can do it for someone else one day." Off we went - both still strangers in that very dark night.

***

Several months later following the flat tire, I was on my way to a day hike on Pacific Crest Trail. As I cruised north on Lake Hughes Road towards my trailhead, a rider on a motorcycle pulled out to pass and was soon out of sight. A few miles later, I noticed a bike that resembled the same one parked alone on the side of the road. "Hmm, wonder what happened to him?"

Soon there he was, looking bedraggled and trekking towards the town in hopes to find help. The little town of Lake Hughes was still about seven miles ahead, and hiking in the heat with a leather jacket and riding boots would soon take its toll on him. The highway was completely deserted, and as I passed him I could see it was the same fellow. He made no attempt to hitch a ride or to summon me for help.

In a somewhat surreal and fleeting moment, the dark night with my flat tire and the words: "Maybe you can do it for someone else one day" haunted me, even though I knew to never pick up strangers on deserted roads. Somehow the situation came together, and that little voice in my head said: "Richard, it's OK! Help the man as he might do for you."

I stopped, backed up at least a dozen yards and asked: "Can I give you a lift?"

I thought he'd near cry; he then said: "you sure can; I've run out of gas and left my can at home; gauge failed, and I ran out." Knowing I would need to postpone my hike, I invited him in and off we drove towards the town to seek help. Later that day, my hike was the best one ever.

XIII

Ports in the storms 2021

Prelude

I find it an unusual coincidence that *Ports in the storms* just happens to be the same chapter number (13) as it is in *For all too soon*. No, truly, I didn't plan it that way but I am fascinated by it nonetheless. There it represents life in the post adolescent time of spring. Here, it takes a full turn in fall. The principle is the same, but life since that time has provided a duel view. Ports in the storms still provide comfort; but mostly, the possibility that we ourselves may have been a refuge for others in ways that we were not aware of at the time.

Let us begin with the introductory excerpt from Page 109 of *For all too soon* called "The lighthouse."

The lighthouse (Excerpt reprint)

"I do hope, dear reader, that I have not bored you with technical stories that may be of no interest to you. But my adventures are my memoirs as well, and remain a part of me. I would like to think that such things might even be similar circumstantially to some of your own, even though we surely must have different points of reference. For example, each of us has reached for some lifeline at one time or another: a familiar street when you may be lost; the comfort of waking up in your own bed after a dream of being alone and confused; a friend, spouse, or parent when [we are] stricken with grief, all become *beacons* at times of stress. The little red light on the water tower back in winter – the one in my first trailer park at about age four – was my first non-human beacon. It was the one that told me when I was to return home to safety."

Impressions

Andrew was a very special student who came to me in the early days of our *Braille Music Division* at SCCM. It was during the hopeful expansion of our large estate campus that later ended due to failed attempts to acquire city permits to continue. Little Andrew was only six years old at that time. He was a delightful young gentleman, and very quick to learn the rigors of reading music in braille. He concurrently studied piano with my partner, Grant, while I coached and taught him to read music. He was blind from birth, yet always had a cheerful smile to brighten any teacher's day.

By time he turned about nine years old, we began to present him in the Royal Conservatory of Music examination programs. His piano teacher often hosted the annual events at our campus. The first year, he placed with a top score above all the sighted students from the Southern California area. SCCM had entered 12 students in the program that year. Six of those were blind, and all placed with the highest scores.

After seven years, SCCM gave up the estate campus due to economic downturns, and leased a small facility in another location. Andrew followed us there and continued to study well into his teens until the school closed after a fifty year life.

Time went by. One day I received a call from Andrew. It was his first night in the resident dorm at UCLA. He seemed rather lost and in need of some familiar company, as it may have been the first time he was alone and away from his family. I was, indeed, flattered that he chose to call me. We talked for quite a while, and I truly felt as though I had become his *port in a storm* that night.

More time had passed when I received an email message from Andrew. He had now graduated with his degree in political science and wanted to share that news. But mostly, he expressed how much Grant and I had meant to him in his life.

* * *

Richard had just turned ten years old when a knock on his mother's front door brought the news that his father had just gone down in a fiery plane crash. Dad and his student pilot had perished just hours before in the Cessna 140 aircraft (*For all too soon* - "Winter," Page 18).

The following morning Doc, my dad's best friend and a loving big brother to me, learned the news and came to comfort us. Much was to follow during the next few days, but I clearly remember him with his arms around mom and me quietly saying all that he could think of at that moment which was, "you poor kids; what to do now, what to do?" Doc would remain our helper and a boy's best friend and companion from that time forth.

* * *

My mother braved it alone and went to work when dad's insurance money ran out. She never left any stone unturned in the effort to make a fine home and safe refuge for me while growing up. I'd often awaken during the night with dreams of crashing airplanes worsened by the sound of air raid sirens being tested during the Cold War. She was there in every way for me, while always holding herself up dealing with her own grief and loss of my father.

She re-married after I graduated high school, and later I married at age 24. Following my divorce and the passing of my stepdad, mom became ill.

Her first stroke occurred one night while I was still at work teaching lessons at the music store. I left immediately, and by time I was able to get to her, the ambulance had already taken her to emergency care. I walked into the bustling hospital to where I was told she was resting. The look of joy with tears in her eyes just to see me, was like a long lost reunion. She smiled as though hoping to take the worry from me. Just like another story in *Winter*, she said: "are you OK?" It was then that I realized it was now my turn to be her *port in that storm*.

* * *

When Richard first moved to his new mobile home in 1990, it was to him like a miracle to ever own a home again, especially after leaving most material things and a home behind in a divorce. I called it "The Other Miracle on 34th Street," based on a 1947 movie (*For all too soon*, Page 211) about a child's Christmas wish.

As years passed, the *miracle* was taken over by a corporation of investors. Site rents for mobile homes soared ruthlessly by nearly $500 a month increase in just a few years. The park became quite run down with new hopeful buyers turned off and out-priced.

In about 2010, a greedy developer began an effort to close down the once prestigious little community so as to level mountains and build a kind of self-contained city around it. Hearings were being held, and not wanting to wait until the "other shoe dropped," I purchased a lot by the shores of the troubled Salton Sea. If the park were to close, I would at least have a place to move my home to, although a very expensive and uncertain proposition in itself.

Well, things have settled somewhat as to 34th Street closing. However, selling is now nearly prohibitive with costs to buy increasing and lot rent inflated to beyond most buyers' means. But no matter, Richard's own lot at Salton Sea Beach sits waiting. It will remain his port in this storm for the *someday* saga - and another miracle - to play out.*

**How strange it is that the street address of the lot at Salton Sea Beach begins with the number 34...*

* * *

Epilogue

For those who may have read my spring through summer remembrance, some of these stories may seem familiar. But they have now played out, or perhaps shall I say, *matured* in their effect on my later life, and do remain an active catalyst. As said before, each of our own stories may become anyone's story thus is how history is written. If any of it should strike a familiar place or *port* within you as a reader, it would be wonderful to one day let the author know. A strange request to come from within a kind of life novel, but is it not true that many novels, plays, songs, and movies often become a reader's bond with a writer they have never met?

I will conclude *our* chapter with a second look at what I feel is one of the most powerful love stories of mutual comfort that has ever occurred in my life. The story is that of one between the author and a fellow creature - not unlike the special communication between a pet and its master at a time when the animal's end of life may be near. Let this remain with you always as a lesson when lost and all hope seems gone.

> *The following is an excerpt from my remembrance through summer, called "The heart of a coyote" found on pages 154-155. The family I refer to was that of my spouse prior to our separation.*

"On one of my last outings with the family, we had made a trip to the Los Angeles Zoo. By then I began feeling somewhat like an outsider, but nevertheless was included that day.

"As we entered the beginning of the zoo tour, a caged animal caught my attention. It was a lone coyote – completely out of place as I'd come to know them. I stopped for a moment to sit by the cage, watching the neurotic animal across the far end of his unnatural confines. I was completely taken with the piercing look in his eyes. He immediately made eye contact with me, staring in a way that seemed to penetrate deep into the inner places of my soul. It seemed in one way unearthly; and yet in another, a reaching out.

"Someone became impatient and said something like: Are you going to sit there all day with that mangy animal or come with the rest of us? I responded that they should just go ahead and I would catch up with them shortly. Off they went, probably just as glad to be rid of me for a while as my company was not pleasant at that juncture.

"The time was near noon; a short while later they came back to where they left me wondering what happened. There I was still sitting with the caged coyote that had edged his way close to the screen that separated us. We clearly bonded during that time and somehow became one in spirit. Perhaps it was now my turn to understand [share] his heartache, and to wonder why he was imprisoned as an object only for curiosity seekers to gaze upon."

XIV

Dreams

Chapter thirteen was more about being lost and finding a *port* of refuge - that familiar place of assurance and comfort that we have all reached for at one time or another. Such is true of man or perhaps even *el coyote*. So you see why this might even be your story as lived through my experiences, perhaps a *shared remembrance* in a manner of speaking.

Dreams somehow seem to emerge from personal exposures and that which has been, or is currently on a person's mind. Allow me now to share some of them from my own past memories. Perhaps you will adjust the subconscious picture and apply the general predicaments as you wish. Think of each pageant as a play of actors, that is a kind of microcosm complete within itself. It matters not what might have been the stimuli, and yet they remain private within our own personal worlds. (OK; no fair trying to psychoanalyze the author; but do look into the mirror - smiles.)

The hotel

You are attending a conference out of town at perhaps a Marriott, or other convention center. You've arrived following your journey, register, and are in process of bringing luggage into the refuge of a quiet and peaceful room. "Boy, that steak and bottle of good wine that I planned on my first night before workshops begin tomorrow, sure sounds good!"

Activities such as lunch, becoming familiar with places you will frequent - exhibit halls, banquets, etc., now occupy your afternoon. Upon returning towards your room you suddenly stop in your tracks feeling rather strange; you become disoriented, alone, and frightened: "What floor was my room on? What was the room number?" Nothing seems to look familiar. "Oh well, I'll just go to the registration desk and ...; but without details, will they be able to help? I forgot my ID. Aw shit!"

Hallway after hallway looks the same; floor after floor, the elevator seems to be in a different place. You see a familiar door, open it expecting an elevator, but find it's only a broom closet. On it goes until you - shaking - wake up. It was only a dream.

The parked car

Just before sundown, you've ventured into an unfamiliar and rather dense neighborhood for a meeting after dark. Your car is neatly parked on a street along with a sea of other vehicles. It is somewhat out of the conscious mind as you seek your destination for the visit of the evening. Hours later you walk out into the darkness and head for your carriage to begin the trip home.

Confident that your mind's GPS will remember where you parked, you walk, and walk, and walk. "It looks like...; it should be right over...;" but nothing looks the same. Hours of searching and hoping only bring fear and bewilderment.

Suddenly you recognize a familiar shape, breathe a sigh, and head for it only to find it's sort of, kinda', like, but not the right one. More walking and frustrated, you spot - what you think is - your *port* only to find it up on blocks, wheels stolen, and hopelessly vandalized.

The Sportsman's Inn

During my experimental venture into the world of Real Estate, I was tending to a kind of *eagles roost* listing high up in the hills above the San Fernando Valley. This particular afternoon, I met a young lady agent from another office who often frequented her clients in the same community. I knew of her from other times and always enjoyed chatting with her about our work.

As it turned out, like me she also had another career - that of teaching the interpretation of dreams in classes at a local community college. We traded some college teaching experiences that day, and I happened to mention a recurring dream that I was having with respect to my then recent and difficult divorce. She asked me if I could remember any familiar threads concurrent with each of those dreams.

"Yes, as a matter of fact. I chance to meet her on a band break while playing a gig in the restaurant lounge."

"And ..."

"Well, she always seems to be wearing a black blouse. Seems kinda' curious, but not sure why."

"What does black mean to you?"

"Mourning, I suppose. Could it be that she's...?"

"Most likely not. To me it means that *you* have finally accepted that she is no more. A kind of death or closure has come to a grim, but liberating reality in your subconscious."

"Hmmm."

Home fires

It has been at least forty years since you left your parents warm home - married, divorced, and many lifetimes later. Mom and stepdad passed away at least thirty of those years before, and life goes on.

Suddenly out of nowhere, you find yourself driving up a familiar driveway - a home that you grew up in before leaving the nest. A front door opens, and mom - as familiar a port as always - steps out and greets you. No one else lives there now as dad is long past, but home fires and the glow of light inside eagerly await you as though you were expected

- a kind of surreal time-warp of sorts. You are overwhelmed with warm memories and await a home-cooked meal and the familiar energy inside.

As you awaken with an abrupt start to a place and time that you cannot yet recognize, with sleepy eyes you fall into a deep heartache, weeping, and very alone in the reality of *now*.

Little Dream Vignettes

Late returning home, you stop to find a phone booth. Near panic, you know that your loved one is home alone, waiting, waiting, and terribly worried. Newly married, you agonize to think she may be sick with worry and wondering why you haven't called: "just a few miles more and I'll be closer, I know."

Dialing the phone while shaking with anxiety, you try several times. Each time you get to the last number you miss-dial it. Anxiously, the number becomes scrambled in your mind and you have no way to make contact with the most important person in your life.

Newly married, a young music teacher works at the academy with his students. Each day, he anticipates his arriving home to open arms, a warm familiar smile and wonderful new wife. The newlyweds have been a little family for only six months.

It is ca. 1969. A young boy student, still somewhat intermediate in his learning, is working patiently with simple folk and pop music so as to build harmony and fingerboard geography for what is to come. The youngster has chosen to learn the song, "Honey" for his chord work this week.

Teacher - softly playing and singing the song for his student to hear - arrives at the lyric that describes where his lady has passed away in the early spring following their wedding.

"Mr. _____," queries the boy, "you have some tears in your eyes; why is that?"

Over and over, and over again he dreams of a labor-intensive effort to explain a simple musical concept to a class or to a private adult student. He becomes obsessed to succeed and to bathe in the joy of watching the students grasp the idea. His reward is to see that ever familiar light of "yes" in their faces. After all, it does sometimes happen that way.

The dream never seems to have closure, which is to complete the effort. It just goes on, and on, and on, again and again with the explaining just fading away. He now awakens exhausted and just glad it's over - this time.

Gratitude, Ignorance, & Philosophy

Prologue

In *For all too soon,* Richard shared his experiences, adventures, growing up years, and many things that came to be well before he had any idea that - one day - he might write them into a story. In *Summer's Memory,* all has come to pass from that time. As said before, *leave the past behind, and you might well risk stumbling into your future.* [*For all too soon*, Introduction, Page ix]

Much of what you read now was still in my future then. However, such reflects an updated version along with some increased senior courage to be blunt. Stumbled into or not, the present season was reached by my own private roads paved directly to the *now* that I've come to know. So be prepared for some humble views and some opinions. Remember too that, age and mileage - right or wrong in one's estimation, carries frankness and sometimes a bit of a well-earned attitude. As with an experienced optimist, a bit of pessimism now and then tends to strengthen the *former* and to temper the *latter.*

* * *

To be a good student is to have faith, humility, and gratitude

In an earlier chapter, I wrote about certain methods and strategies that experienced music teachers apply initially may not always seem to be the direction in which a student desires to go.

Many teachers prefer to not teach older students. Adults (even very young adults) will sometimes question a teacher's methods due to their own premature self-evaluation to make such judgments. After a time, should such a student move on to what seems (qualified or not) a "better" teacher, he or she might express that ...*the last teacher was not teaching me properly*. Such statements have even been seen on social media.

What some students may fail to realize is that they were not yet qualified at the time to recognize why a teacher used a method he or she did. By abandonment of that teacher, they may never see their own lack of musical maturity or face their own part in why they were not progressing. Just as a parent might talk to a pubescent child in ways that they understand at their age, the music teacher must conduct his or her instruction to the current and expanding level of the student. Sure, we grow and become more sophisticated in our skills, but as with most new knowledge, we may still lack the experience to best apply it. As such, we sometimes know just enough to be very dangerous to ourselves. Do remember that, unlike the common implication for the word *ignorance*, it does NOT mean stupid, defective, or myopic. It simply means *lacking knowledge or experience*. [Webster's *New World Dictionary* - Pocket-Size Edition]

Lesson: Ask your teacher why he or she is using an approach that you are confused about. Admit that you may one day know the reason, but have some discomfort now. Restate your original goal! But whatever you do, know that once that teacher is in your musical past, he or she will never have the chance to remind you of what you didn't know then, and how it could have affected outcome. Your so called "better" teacher may very well be a good self-promoter, but less experienced in methodology. By applying your own evaluation of the moment prematurely, you have *stumbled* into your future, risked your potential, and perhaps traded your innocent faith for a very bumpy road ahead.

Now for the philosophy stuff

Clearly, Richard's autumn season is not meant to morph into a past, present, or future treatise only on his personal views about music and/or education. But so much that I see in today's trends that might affect - in my humble opinion - tomorrow's learners, seems counterproductive to that which has been gained from our traditional ways of life. Consequently, learning, recreation, and the ever changing *yin, yang* have become rather sharply scrutinized in the September of my own years. This view was never present in quite the same way in my winter through summer seasons. Why is that? Could it be that Richard was still learning too?

One example I want to offer is that of an excerpt from the *Preliminary Thoughts for Students and Teachers of Music Braille* found in my publication, *An Introduction to Music for the Blind Student,* Teachers' Handbook.

Edited excerpt follows: (Page X - © Copyright 2009, Reprint with permission)

GENERAL PHILOSOPHY

"Many things have been accomplished in recent times to further the cause of literacy for blind music students. Computer software to help the music transcriber and braille music translation software represent some of the wonderful advancements in support of our students. An upsurge in certified transcribers in recent years has dramatically contributed to critically needed resources. Never before has The Library of Congress produced so many fine and dedicated music transcribers. Braille production for music is perhaps the highest in history. And although the pool of professional transcribers remains small, technology creates opportunities never before thought possible. Music transcribers can now take their place along with other professionals to earn a respectable living at their craft.

"Yet there is still so much to be done in order to better educate the educators. While the technology, production, awareness, and implementation of music braille literacy has made striking advances, the science of educating those who use and teach these skills has virtually stood still if not regressed.

"For example, if you plan to teach math in the school system, your credential must reflect math as your specialty. If you plan to teach music, your degree will most likely be in music education. And if you plan to teach visually impaired students, your credential will focus on VI special education. If you desire to teach any academic skill to blind students be it math, music, law, or whichever, your education will require intense study in those areas.

"Conversely, if you plan to specialize in music braille disciplines for blind music students - whether they are college-bound or not - you may be surprised to learn that [with respect to music braille pedagogy] (as of this publication date [2009]), there is no training, no credential, no requirement whatsoever built into the music education major no matter which school you choose to attend.

"The Library of Congress has been certifying music transcribers for many decades. No one has ever certified a music braille educator. Is it then any wonder why we seem to have fallen behind in this important area of music education itself? Can anyone justify a college who would graduate a student – blind or sighted – with a music degree while allowing him or her to remain musically illiterate? And yet, with respect to the blind music student, schools, universities, and colleges may have un-intentionally fostered such a history."*

A significant change has occurred since that time, in that few colleges or universities will accept a blind student into a music program without a working knowledge of reading music braille. However, teacher certifications are still not addressed, nor are any prerequisites or solutions defined for incoming candidates.

A bit of philosophy on the lighter side

Often, trends and attitudes can be observed while eavesdropping on conversational dialogue between individuals - somewhat like "the fly on the wall."

The following short rhetorical scenarios are meant for fun, and the characters are fictional. However, the concepts are clearly inspired philosophically. Some come from real trends and events that Richard has either observed during these autumn years, contemplated, or probably felt the hair on his back raising not unlike a domestic cat unexpectedly meeting a wild raccoon whilst thinking: "What the hell is **that?**"

Two tech cynics out for lunch

"John, what do you think about some of the revelations on extraterrestrial discoveries as of late?" [Ethan]

"It's all bullshit to me, as we can't even keep our proverbial stuff together here on our own planet." [John]

"My sentiment exactly! I mean why in heaven's name is there such a push to conquer outer space anyway?" [Ethan]

"That's easy," grins John as his Martini also begins to grin. "*Space Exide* just wants to get up there as soon as possible so as to set up shop before the satellite boom smothers the earth, and leaves no rocket corridors for getting through their orbits."

"John, that sure figures. I didn't think that it might be for the good of mankind, now would it?"[Ethan]"

Blessed are the meek for they shall inherit the earth*

Pastor: "I've always loved that one, as it gives comfort and dignity to the less fortunate, and some hope as well."

Brother Meek: "I guess; but why did you bring that up here in the beer gardens, Father?"

Pastor while slowly sipping: "Well, you are a beautiful example of doing much with very little - a true salt of the earth. Wouldn't you like to inherit the planet and live like the rich?"

Bro. Meek: "No f...n' way, Padre! - Too many landfills." Gulp.

*(from *The Beatitudes, #3* - found in the Christian bible)

Turnabout

"Jim, you're a good and honest businessman; what would be your thought on how to defeat a *take-and-give-nothing* corporation such as the one we've been talking about?"

"Well, they're a large slum-lord type of investment group. What I would do is to buy three mobile homes in one of their parks then put the group in my will!"

'What! Why in god's name would you do that after the ruthless way that they have treated some tenants?"

"Think about it! I'd fix the titles so there's a long battle over liens, then forever look down and watch 'em go bankrupt while they continue to lose rent 'cause they can't sell 'em with clouds on the title, and because the space rent is way too high."

"What if you outlive them?"

"I'll call the liens due, file Chapter 11 then contact their liquidators."

RICHARD E. TAESCH

Digital blasphemy

> *An imagined (tongue-in-cheek) presentation given by a guest speaker at a retirement dinner for old typewriter repairmen:*

"Good evening ladies and gentleman! My name is Dr. Phu Lin Yu. I would like to offer a few - rather biased - opinions on what I call *out of control* technology.

"I often wish that others might one day see what some of us saw coming so long ago. It's strawberry fields, Zoom relationships, virtual emptiness everywhere, and yet it only gets worse. No one sees it but a few of us who were paying attention to such things before anyone heard of them. Nowadays, if we don't buy into every new upgrade, we're considered tech-challenged and behind the trends. E.g., raise your hands if you did not know that the original USB plugs are already considered obsolete; or that some folks really think the *Cloud* is something in the sky meant to house one's computer files, and that it is protected by Jesus.

"And the beat goes on, but no one can hear it, as that is digitized too. To talk to one of the 'tech disciples, one must surely be silently thinking that ...*What you do speaks so loudly that I cannot hear what you say.** That is because *fact* is now virtual too, which also requires a password. And *what you say* gets more difficult to hear when one is talking to someone on an Internet phone. It seems that the more wonderful things that the new phones can do, the worse the audio gets. *(Emerson)

"As said, progress is not *always* a good thing as disease also progresses. When I was a kid, we used tin cans with strings stretched between them. The audio was a hell sight better than most phones today where the rap is agonizing to the fellow on the other end. It sounds like someone talking to you from the bottom of an old beer can.

"It simply ain't going the right way folks! I knew that long before anyone would have accused us simple-minded rebels of *digital blasphemy*."

Saving for one's old age

This conversation often came up between a small college dean and one or two of her curious colleagues. Miss Martin would usually avoid the sensitive subject of why her rather wealthy family had never contributed endowment funds to her school. After all, the question was hard to avoid when the school was always short of support. Moreover, President Myra Martin's billionaire family could surely use such the tax advantage as well as the others that they were known to invest in.

Over lunch one afternoon, Dr. Charles Norton, professor of psychology, seized the relaxed mood and asked her:

"Dean Martin, have you ever proposed a formal request to your sister's foundation for our school? After all, she is world known in her profession and should surely care about her family's accomplishments."

"Well, Dr. Norton, I've quite often hinted at the idea, but as soon as the word *music* comes up she usually changes the subject."

'That just doesn't make sense, Myra - uh, you don't mind me using your first name, I hope - ...."

"No, *Chuck*; but what would be your suggestion?"

Meanwhile, Professor Kronic suddenly interrupts while playing with the croutons on his salad. "Yes, Myra, what about that?"

"Ah, Jack," echoes Charles, "just what is *your* take?"

"Look, gentlemen," injects Myra. "Just last month I asked my sister Myrna point blank, what might be the reason for never considering the college as a possibility for contributing to an endowment for us."

"Yes, and what was her answer, if any?"

"She said that she was saving it for her old age."

"Well, ... Myra, if you don't mind my asking, how old is Mrs. Stewart?"

"She's 93."

XVI

Routes of passage

Prologue / Prelude

In *For all too soon*, I wrote much about my own boyhood in the spring season chapters. So much of that time and the joys that it brought into my life, were clearly due to experiencing what is called *rites of passage*. I sometimes call them *routes of passage* instead. They are those significant *rites, ceremonies, or pathways* that become preludes to new gradient levels, or *passage* into each next maturity. Here, I will refer only to the little things, but such may be no little thing at all depending on one's life experience and exposure at any given time.

In one definition of the term *rites of passage*, Webster's says: "...an event in a person's life regarded as having great significance" [Webster's New World Dictionary, Third College Edition]. These *events* need not be any more significant than the simple act of learning to ride a bicycle. Or perhaps roller-skating on Friday nights in hopes to one day meet that special one, then savoring the act of holding hands when meeting again (as opposed to jumping into bed on the first date). In *For all too soon*, I wrote about the simpler times and some of those little joys thus:

SUMMER'S MEMORY

> *The times before acquiring our first cars were perhaps the best times of our lives. Our world was smaller, and exploration of it was to us as exciting as traveling the world is for many of the more fortunate young people of today. As I observe my students at the same age as I was at certain points, I marvel at the fact that few do not have Smart Phones, new cars, and have seen and done it all before age 18. In many ways I pity them, as I truly believe that simple joys found in rites of passage have been denied them.*

Yes, I must say that my autumn years as pondered in this writing, have provided far more appreciation and understanding for the value of such rites of passage from my youth than I could possibly have known at that time. Mostly, I was just much too involved with growing up and looking ahead to even recognize or define such a concept. In other words, as kids we were too busy living life to notice the process.

Nothing is really that much different for youth growing up in today's digital world. But one thing does seem to be missing - that of the unparalleled joy of *Routes of Passage* - the little journeys that were not at all *little* in our eyes then.

In the following vignettes, I will share some of my autumn season impressions of those simpler times. Some of them will reflect a growing up in a very humble way as to material things; not necessarily poverty, hunger, or deprivation, just plain simple ways. Most of us in my circle had loving families. But very few had the luxury items such as owning their own home, as we rented. Or perhaps steaks once a week instead of Mac 'n Cheese, a new family car every year, and so on. Other vignettes will share some things that I have observed, such as those older folks who remain childlike and *simple* in their own rite.

* * *

Untitled Vignettes

While shopping in a market produce area one afternoon, I noticed a senior citizen curiously poring over the avocado section with great interest and curiosity. While I pretended to not to notice, I could see him carefully picking one of them up while examining the strange-looking fruit on all sides - holding it as though in various light sources.

"Jeez," I thought, "how interesting; surely he must have seen an avocado before! Well, perhaps he's a market buyer, or just quite expert in proper selection - hmmm, they are sometimes hard to pick just right. Ah well Richard, just get on with why you came in here."

Suddenly, the fellow summons the attention of a young man working in the produce department, stocking, sorting, and such.

"Young man, may I ask you a question?"

"Yeah, but I am kinda' busy now."

"Thank you so much son!" as he holds up one of the dubious items: "What is this?"

The boy turns, eyes wide as if not sure how to respond. After all, everybody surely knows an avocado when they see it; even old guys with fading vision.

"Dude, that's an avocado!"

"But," replies the man quite politely: "how does one eat it and what does it taste like?"

"Uh, well, uh..." with hesitation, "Uh, well it, uh, ya' know ... it, it tastes like an avocado!"

Obviously the question was well over the young man's head. Apparently, he had never had to answer such a thing, and was at a loss himself as to just what is an "avocado." After all, guacamole dip at *El Tacomole* Mexican restaurant following a Margarita or two, was perhaps all that he ever knew.

This, my dear reader, is a simple description of routes of passage. Both the shopper and the produce employee had much to contemplate after that day.

SUMMER'S MEMORY

My home in Van Nuys while growing up after the loss of my dad was a lovely two bedroom house situated on a lot shared by another house of the same type. I was about 12 or 13 years old, and quite used to the summer temperatures without ever hearing of such a thing as air conditioning (AC). We braved it, and even with my old tube-type ham radio gear which generated its own dissipated heat, somehow it was just the way it was and simply a part of the times.

One day mom and I were mulling about a furniture store on Van Nuys Boulevard when she spotted the ultimate solution for taming some of that summer heat. There it sat on a display: For a hefty price of twenty-five dollars, one could bring home a genuine portable evaporative - otherwise known as a swamp - cooler that was guaranteed to bring down the temperature in a single room by at least 2 degrees! All one had to do was to visit the unit every hour and pour a quart of water into the top of it. Voila! AC it was - in 1955, or so. As long as one stood directly in front of the unit, it would be no less than heavenly.

Mom and a close family friend discussed the investment and decided that a monthly payment of $5.00 would be well worth the interest of about ten percent per month. (Family *friend* did spend much time visiting in the warm evenings - a special interest perhaps?) Nonetheless, the purchase was made and the little unit clearly made a difference in our lives. Thus, another *route of passage* into the world of high finance was gained for Richard's future.

I was about twelve years old, and living in the little house told of earlier. My mother and I had made special plans for a long awaited trip to Catalina Island with close friends, which included my - now grown up - childhood playmate, Charlotte. (See the winter story in *For all too soon.*)

It was the night before we were to leave and meet the others for our steamship trip to Avalon Bay as we finished packing and attending to last minute details. Bedtime was a bit overdue, and sleepy eyes anxiously awaited a restful sleep in anticipation of the adventure before us. Low and behold, as Richard began preparing his room for bed, a large awkward flying insect buzzed to and fro around the ceiling lamp. "Drat," says I, "I can't sleep with that thing in here as it must be a mosquito - just what I need! Maaaaa ..." I anxiously beckoned.

I summoned my mom, as she always seemed to have a calm way to usher such visitors out without harming them. As for me, I just stood on the bed not unlike a housewife who just saw a mouse. I then waited for mom to do her magic, armed with a soft dust mop and much patience. At this point, the mosquito identity was (so we thought) confirmed, and the pursuit began.

Now well after midnight, and knowing that neither of us would be worth much for a rested trip in the morning, we chased, evaded, and tried to coax the *invader* with the mop to exit an open window. On and on the time marched and the chase continued. Well, at last the skirmish was won by *Admiral Duster*, and bed was in order. The steamship trip next day was wonderful, and the two weeks of friends and events on the island of romance went as we had hoped.

Well, after surviving that rite of passage, many years later we discovered that our little friend who monopolized our plans before the trip was no mosquito at all!

"Ya' mean we went through all of that for a harmless *whatever it was*?"

Yup! The lanky and clumsy little flying fortress is known as a *Mosquito Hawk,* or sometimes called *Mosquito Bandit.* They are often swatted in error by folks who mistake them for *skeeters.* But in fact - second only to bats - they are the archenemy of the mosquito as they are known to help control the vector population.

So once again recalling my many passages as a boy, I ask (as in Chapter 9 of *For all too soon),* why is it that: *what man cannot seem to control, he so often destroys*?

Bravo for mom, the *dust mop warrior* who won the struggle, and once again *took the hill* without a casualty!

Late one evening just before dark, my friend and I hiked slowly up the narrow trail from the base of the Devil's Punchbowl scenic canyon preserve. It had been a long trek down, then up and out of the canyon to Pacific Crest Trail and the national forest boundary. On the last lap of the return hike, Victoria was growing quite weary. However, the trooper that she was, just put one foot in front of the other making the steep ascent while keeping that tasty pizza we planned to stop for as encouragement. For me, the schooner of beer that I planned on worked wonders.

I was in much awe, as a modest swarm of bats at sundown excited me. I made the attempt to chat with her about their merits, and cited the many myths that society has put upon them. She wasn't terribly impressed, but tolerated my rather bizarre love for the little maligned creatures. (See Chapter IX, "Why is that?" in *For all too soon.*)

Suddenly without warning, a medium-sized bat swarmed down so close to her that she could feel the swish of its wing on her face. Needless to add, she screamed in fear. When I told her what it was she just kept walking as if in disbelief. She never mentioned the experience again.

Several years later the subject came up. In light conversation, I asked if she remembered that event.

"Richard, you do know that I really don't like bats."

"Yes, Victoria, I do; but just for me, take a moment to think about this: What sometimes appears to many misinformed folks that bats will attack people, is just not true. Bats are not known to attack people. Mosquitoes attack people! The night that we were hiking up from the Punchbowl, most likely a mosquito was honing in very close and about to take sample of blood from your lovely face. The bat was probably honing in on him, not you. Victoria, that little creature that you do not like may very well have saved your life!"*

*Outtake

In Austin Texas there is a bridge that tourists flock to each year to witness thousands of bats that swarm from under it each night. It is said that, in just one such swarm, bats can consume enormous quantities of disease-causing mosquitoes. Not to mention that they are perhaps one of the most prolific pollinators on the earth, and significantly support our food supply. Moreover, very few people have ever been known to contract or succumb to bat-related diseases.

In recent times, more than one highly acclaimed medium has had its journalistic hands slapped by scientists for engaging in incomplete and misinformed reporting on bats during the Covid pandemic.

Bats are essential to human survival, and yet they have been exterminated and driven to near extinction out of unfounded fear. Why is that?

Visit: *Merlin Tuttle's Bat Conservation*

*See the Video on the Austin experience:
https://youtu.be/fvjDIQPNZTo

XVII

Karma

As we look back over past seasons and our many *routes of passage*, the current view from one's autumn can bring new or enhanced perspectives on certain experiences. As such, we can often learn how to better deal with them on an emotional and social basis. Admit it or not, aging and maturity can slowly bring more truth and reality to many situations - those that may have just been set aside due to unconscious forms of denial.

As to *karma*, Webster's defines it as: "... the totality of one's acts in each state of one's existence." As to human applications, one wonderful quote follows:

> How people treat you is their karma. How you react is yours.
> - Wayne Dyer

This chapter - in my own point and view - needs little introduction, as it should very clearly present its purpose. Most of the names of the actors are fictionalized but the stories are not. Some may even be about *Mr. Tish* in disguise. May the reader simply apply his or her own meanings. Said before, as a member of the human predicament, these could be your stories as well.

RICHARD E. TAESCH

VIGNETTES

Although mostly retired now, Jason still depends on part time income to meet expenses that exceed the monthly SSA benefit. The Covid debacle took quite a toll on many such folks, as closures, etc., reduced or terminated much of their supplemental income.

Having always been quite independent, Jason avoided asking for help from family. When all had passed away, he resisted the option to apply for unemployment benefits. Being formally retired, he had little desire to pursue regular work after 55 years as an accountant. Becoming a rather tired warrior, he preferred to wait until his part time work might resume in a limited way.

With no end in sight, and food costs becoming his most expensive outlay other than home expenses, Jason opted to apply to a food assistance program for benefits. This program is now a special branch of welfare meant to assist retired, disabled, or survivor folks on limited income. (It has been said that in 2022, inflation was higher than in the prior 40 years, and continues to soar in 2024.)

One evening, he was checking out groceries. He then swiped his treasured card at the check stand. Suddenly, he glanced up and noticed the gentleman next in line watching him intensely with what looked like an uneasy attitude. Jason turned away and the discomfort soon dissipated.

The following week while exiting the same store with his weekly purchases, the same man appeared and stopped Jason in the parking lot while approaching his car to load groceries.

"Sir, that sure is a fine looking automobile that you have there; what year is it?" He continued to create what appeared to be friendly interest.

"Oh thank you very much! It's a 1957 *Coupe de Ville*."

"Well, it surely must be nice; especially when using food stamps!" smiled the stranger arrogantly, as though hoping to encourage some kind of self-reflection.

"Excuse me," responded Jason as he wheeled around from packing his groceries, directly facing the man and making eye contact with him.

Obviously, Jason was completely caught off guard and deeply affected. Gently and calmly, he replied in an almost reflexive tone:

"My wife and I bought this car in 1967 for one thousand dollars! We made payments of $30.50 per month until paid. When she passed away, I waited for over thirty years to restore and to have it painted. This is all I drive and rarely at that."

"Oh, I am so sorry, I had no idea that you ... ..."

Having lost patience with such things resulting from other events of late, and still recovering from an illness earlier, Jason interrupts: "Not a problem sir, I'm sure. However, I will leave you hopefully for the last time, and with a lesson: There's an old Indian saying that goes something like: 'Never pass judgment on a person unless you have walked in his [or her] moccasins!' Now may I say God bless you, and better luck with harassing your next less fortunate person!" The man silently turned and walked slowly away.

As said, one is never too old to experience new *routes of passage*.

> *Disclaimer:* Out of fear that I refer to this state of being just one too many times, my apologies go to one or two folks that come to mind. However, may I respectfully submit that we consider another's moccasins at least once before stepping into a similar swamp. Should a moccasin happen to fit, try it on. (The above story is partially fiction, but compassionately inspired.)
>
> But do take heed dear reader: This chapter is about karma, and this version of one person's old emotion just happens to be a fine, although not so pleasant story about damaged spirits, otherwise known in this example as his **karma**.
>
> The following story is simply intended as a lesson in bad karma on my part. Perhaps read the last sentence first, as a lesson in the art of ... pause and reflect.

Richard's programs ended when the failed SCCM closed following fifty years of troubled existence. At that point, there was no choice but to continue some kind of work from home. All school income was now gone, and few options were left. Even with three certifications in the field of braille transcription, I had never intended to become a career braillist.

The purpose at the time of building the SCCM *Braille Music Division* was to educate, and to serve well beyond that of what is called "disposable braille" for class work. Such is often discarded each new semester to be replaced with newer editions. My quest was to provide for our students and other schools in the district, reaching out to as many blind students, their teachers, and families as possible. I would then move aside, allowing full-time transcribers the work that they needed to survive.

But alas, I scrounged an outdated computer to continue transcribing for private schools and alternate media agencies so as to put food on the proverbial table - not unlike the Pied Piper tooting a flute for his dinner. Moreover, there were no personal funds to obtain high speed Internet for the work. I simply asked clients to mail books and materials by regular mail. Any way to print out e-files was out of the question. Archaic *dial-up* for Internet access was all that I could afford.

Perhaps the worst part of this humiliating situation was having to listen to folks that I knew hint at how much easier life will be one day when I *catch up* to the new technology that is currently trending.

Every time I heard someone say: ... oh you have no idea of what you have been missing ..., I wanted to choke. In my school office I had the best there was in state of the art computers that were continuously updated by school technicians. I had multi-networked embossers, and full braille output available that would rival the most well equipped venues that there were. How could anyone know that my pitiful and humble tools now were clearly not my preference. The floor had been completely pulled out from under our (and my partner's) program for the blind, leaving its founders near destitute, and our blind children without the support and technology that no other music school in the world could provide!

On one occasion, I had agreed to help with a sub-contracted transcription project for a colleague and her associate braillist - a transcriber that I had even provided some braille code advice for in the past. The team insisted that they must transmit the files by email as time was short. I told them that my Internet speed would not support the files at this time, and asked if they would simply drop them in the mail for me. I'd be happy to pay the cost. They resisted, and for two days tried numerous attempts to email the work to me. All failed, and time that could easily have worked for the mailing was now exhausted.

At this point with all being frustrated, the associate wrote an email message to me essentially stating: *Richard, I can't waste any more time on someone who cannot keep up with the current technology.*

The project (and badly needed income) was now lost on my end. Along with crushed pride from past history, there was no alternative but to *just eat it up and spit it out.* My moccasins had long worn out, and my troubled feet still ache!

I must admit that my reaction to the sub-contracting associate's karma towards me is a wound that sadly resulted in very bad karma towards him on my part - a wound that might never heal. Other than bad judgment, I still feel that this was not his fault.

There are several aircraft remains left from wrecks high in the San Gabriel Mountains. Sailplane wrecks at high mountain altitudes are less frequent, but have happened at times. One such incident is known to many of the glider pilots who fly from an airport located in the desert foothills below the north face peaks.

As a story seems to go, the pilot loved to make a practice of buzzing close to Pacific Crest trail (PCT) hikers as a kind of lark. He would begin a dive toward them on the ridge. When the hikers heard the familiar whistle of the speeding aircraft, they would usually drop to the ground in mortal fear as the plane appeared to be heading straight for them. At the last minute, the pilot would pull up abruptly, gain altitude, then soar back towards the desert airstrip far below.

Apparently, one day he must have misjudged the wind shear and brushed a pine tree with a wingtip while making the dive. He lost control and crashed violently against the ridge, tumbling down into the canyon north of the trail. Naturally, he did not survive. The forest became the final grave for his plane.

This particular day, I was hiking along Pacific Crest Trail on a ridge at about 8,500 feet elevation. As thoughts rambled, I became aware that somewhere on the steep down-slopes of this same trail was the wreck of that ill-fated sailplane from many years before. Suddenly, I abruptly paused in my tracks. For some unknown reason, a rather unearthly feeling came over me; it seemed to be pleading for me to stop at this time and at this place. I began to look around, muttering to myself: "Why is that and what does it mean? Ah well; I think I'll just walk down into this canyon a few yards beyond the trees and see what things look like."

Somewhat forgetting the ghostly experience of a few moments before, I decided to explore the slope just for curiosity. Suddenly, there it was: the debris and framework of the notorious sailplane that crashed decades ago. For a moment, I near froze with fear recalling the unexpected event that had just happened. "Richard, don't think about it; it has nothing to do with this - does it?"

As I began to examine the wreckage, I saw the fuselage with the registration numbers still very readable. The nose cone of the glider had severed with the impact, but parts of the cockpit that the pilot was probably thrown from were quite well preserved. Eerie was an understatement knowing what this was and how it got here. The man's after life energy somehow seemed to haunt me.

As I made my way up the slope to continue my hike, several small pieces of debris became visible under brush and logs. Suddenly, under one log I spotted a shiny object and began to shiver somewhat. I carefully removed the object to find that it was clearly what must have been his glasses. I left all that I found and continued to hike sadly back to my car. The event that follows in the next vignette is a short story of karma resulting from my grisly discovery, one that I will never, ever forget.

I hiked the same PCT trail where I had spotted the glider wreckage many times. I always enjoyed the ascent to the top of Mt. Baden Powell. At the summit, there is a memorial monument to the founder the Boy Scouts of America, Lord Robert Baden Powell.

It was nearing dark on my return trek back towards the trailhead where my car and a thermos of hot coffee lay in wait for me. I was now perhaps about a mile past the cutoff where I discovered the sailplane wreck several months ago. All of a sudden I spotted a large white and familiar item tucked carefully behind a pine tree on my left. Using my flashlight, I was able to see that someone had removed the nose cone from that wreckage, perhaps in an attempt to keep it as a trophy, or just as a keepsake. He most likely became unable to tote it further, as it was quite heavy being composed of fiberglass and a steel frame. Nevertheless, there appeared to be a planned return to complete the mission at another time.

This was just not at all OK with me! In my deepest respect for the sanctity of the pilot's memory, the nose cone had to be returned to the crash site - and not later, but NOW! Weary as I was from the day's hiking, I was determined to carry the item back and ceremoniously replace it where it should remain, at least until someday the wreckage might be officially removed.

Well into the dark I struggled. Bracing the item on my shoulder, I returned deep into the dark canyon gravesite. I then gently placed the nose cone with the wreckage where it had come to rest years ago, knelt, and uttered a prayer. A return to the trailhead at 3 am in the morning and that hot cup of coffee, brought a very pleasant feeling of well-being and "mission accomplished." My karma, and perhaps a part of the deceased pilot's spirit was returned to rest in peace within the quiet forest that memorable night.

Now resting in peace

SUMMER'S MEMORY

MID AUTUMN

XVIII

Millennium meanderings

Overture

As the unfinished last season begins winding down to a trot, a return to the familiar collections of little stories with differing moods and diversified messages seems fitting. Following the Short Stories, I plan to finish Chapter 24 at the end of the book with a finale of one story in the form of a past published article. This will serve as a kind of first and last statement describing one of my favorite causes: that of independence through literacy for all. And fitting it will be, as that treatise was also the beginning of my new found career. My work in the field of music would now include literary freedom for blind musicians, students, and those who teach them. And how fortunate are those of us who have seen our life's work complete one full circle.

SHORT STORIES - Points & Views #7

The two bears

In recent years of my autumn season, I have taken to hiking more close to my home here on 34th Street. Driving into the high country as I loved to do in my summer just became too expensive to travel and maintain the car. However, I am still living within short walking distance from many state park trailheads, so I've come to be quite comfortable in frequenting them regularly.

East Canyon trail is one of my favorites; many an adventure has taken place for me within that wilderness area. One tends to meet fellow hikers and mountain bikers there quite often. Occasionally, a casual chat trading events and animal sightings reveals folks having spotted California black bears in the canyons. My usual skeptic (thoughts, of course) reaction is "no way, this is just too low altitude for bears. I see them in the high forest but never here, not even in thirty years of hiking these trails." Well, guess what?

One such trail goes deep into a canyon only accessible by a rather hidden cutoff. I was trekking along the narrow path which later cuts back up to the top of a mountain at about 2,200 ft. The scenery is quite wild and somewhat resembles far more remote areas. It's truly a very cathartic and deserted bypass away from other hikers and bikes.

I was walking alone this day, allowing rambling thoughts and distractions to remove me from reality. Suddenly, two black bears dashed down from a higher slope to my right directly across my trail, perhaps no more than four feet in front of me. Yikes, I said silently! Having had many similar encounters with wildlife, and forgetting that I would never believe anyone who said they spotted bears in this area, I instinctively stopped walking and just quietly looked at them.

The youngster was freaked out at my presence and promptly climbed up the nearest pine tree. Mom, more freaked out, continued across the trail then turned around down slope from us. She stood on hind feet panting and alternating her looks between the little guy up the tree, and to see what I was going to do. Of course, I wasn't about to do anything at that point but look non-threatening. That seemed to be OK with mom as she just watched intensely. There were no threatening signs from her, so I just slowly and gently pretended to continue my hike, passing the tree that baby was now lodged in and walking as if no big deal.

As soon as I reached the top of a nearby ridge, I stopped and turned hoping not to see one of them following. I could clearly hear her calling in hopes to coax the little fellow down from his refuge in the tree. I began to feel a bit guilty, as poor mom just kept a kind of intermittent and pitiful sounding call to her baby.

Once I reached the top of main trail, I encountered a familiar married couple riding their mountain bikes. I could still hear the calling echoing from down the canyon below while I revealed my story to them as if in disbelief.

"Folks, you won't believe it, but I just had two bears run right across my trail; can you hear that sound? The mother is trying to call the baby bear down from a tree."

"Oh, yeah," the lady replies in a sort of ho-hum fashion; "we see 'em often."

"Well, heck! I was certain there were no bears at this altitude. It's really a surprise!"

"Nah! Happens a lot. You've just never been lucky enough to run into 'em."

"What a privilege; guess one never knows. We are where the wild things are, I suppose."

"Yup! Have a good one."

GPS / GSP or not to be?

Our daily phone visit began with the usual greeting: "Hey Bud! Are you home today?"

"Yo, Bob," I replied. "What's up?"

My friend, Bob, was one of the first special friends that I made while learning to fly sailplanes in the late eighties. As a long time pilot himself, flight instructor (as was my father), and now a part-time tow pilot at the soaring school, we had much in common (music and Amateur Radio too).

"Did you hear on the news today about the commercial plane crash?"

Cringing some from my past history of losing my dad in a crash while teaching someone to fly, I responded cautiously: "No, Bob; what happened?"

"Well, they don't have all the details yet, but from the general description I know exactly what happened."

"What do you mean?"

"Richard, I know that airplane well. It is more than powerful enough to have overcome any headwind even in that bad weather. A pilot should never, never depend on autopilot in weather like that."

"How do you know they were doing that?"

"Son, I just know."

The following few days brought a story that the "black box" found in the cockpit revealed the last conversation between the young woman first officer and her co-pilot.

"Hey Bud; you home today? I just heard the result of the initial investigation. What'd I tell you?" Bob then described a kind of digest of the conversation that the black box contained:

> *Remember the old days when pilots used to really have a challenge navigating a bad storm like this on final approach? Now we just sit back and relax while GPS does all the worrying and takes us all home safely.*
>   - silence....

All fifty passengers, including the pilot and co-pilot, died in that "safe" GPS landing.

The great copper heists

Richard likes to hike regularly in a lovely isolated wilderness beginning just beyond a gate at the end of his street.

I had taken a short evening hike just over the first ridge. I planned to sit peacefully and do some reading in a woodsy kind of meadow bordering the trail. It was now nearing twilight, as I suddenly looked up and across the field to see strangers hiking. They were carrying what appeared to be grappling gear, tools, and other equipment, not unlike that sometimes seen with power-line workers.

This was indeed strange, as not only are there rarely other folks that hike here, but the area has no other access other than my mobile home community. Moreover, I had never seen any of these folks in our park before. There were two or three men with ropes around their shoulders and tools in a waist holster. There were also a couple of women walking dogs, and two children. It almost appeared staged so as to look unnoticed - just a common group of evening hikers that didn't look *common* at all. They suddenly saw me and I just waved back at them as if to not pay any special attention. However, my unexpected appearance did seem to alarm them somewhat.

As the evening sauntered on, I decided to rest for a while following the sunset. The mystery caravan never reappeared, yet I knew that there was no other way out of the old ranch land at the north end. It was almost as if they waited to return, hoping that no one else would see them. They needn't have been carrying clipboards to look suspicious.

About one week later I took the same route. I continued over the ridge for a few miles, then back toward a little canyon before mounting the short trek home. Having crawled into a grotto for a nap, I fell deep asleep. When I awoke it was hours after dark. Before starting back, I broke out my LED so as to check here and there for obstacles in my path.

As I ascended the last short grade to the ridge top in the dark before descending back to the gate, something strange caught my eye that was definitely not in the middle of the same trail earlier that day. The item appeared stranger the closer I came to it. At first, I remembered the little entourage one week before, and wondered if perhaps they had returned and tried to toss a rope over the power line for some reason. The tower was a rather low type as the ridge was one station holding the power lines leading to the next ridge in the distance. The scene appeared to be a playful attempt with a rope end dangling on the ground.

"Oh shit" I exclaimed quietly, "this is the loose end of a cut power line on that tower." There was no other explanation, and I had nearly walked directly into it in the dark. I then remembered that a couple of weeks before, the copper lining had been stolen out of a near new air conditioning unit on our school building roof. There had been a recent trend of copper heists in the area, and many of those were also from power line towers.

I concluded that very likely while I was asleep in the canyon, the operation must have begun. Perhaps the group became spooked while in the midst of the caper, as they may have seen my light in the dark from directly below while I was making my way up to the trail. Not expecting a living soul to be anywhere near there at night, they either aborted the plan or made off with a section of cable. What I came upon was the result. They could have easily exited through the gate and disappeared well before I came near the area in which they were working.

As soon as I arrived home, I phoned our park manager as I knew that she had message access to the power line company to report emergencies. She said she would call, but apparently forgot to do so the following day.

All seemed to be forgotten for about two weeks, as I assumed that Edison had taken care of whatever had occurred. Well, not to be! Sure enough, I looked out of my kitchen window up to the ridge one morning to see smoke coming up right where I had discovered the downed power line. Apparently, the wind was swishing it forth and back and eventually started a brush fire. At first I was certain that any informed thief would have chosen the NOT-live, top center cable used for lightening arrest; apparently this one was quite alive.

Authorities and fire people were called to stop a potentially nasty blaze, and the diagnosis was just as I thought: another attempted copper wire theft. How ironic to think that my flashlight may have saved the thief's life as the wire was alive. Most likely they moved on to another plan, as there was a new fire at another tower in the same canyon about two weeks later, and from the same kind of attempt.

Thanks for helping - but not in my neighborhood - Please!

Amateur Radio was, at one time, a voluntary mainstay backup for civilian and military communication. In times of national and international emergencies, operators would often provide a means to talk with families at home for soldiers and personnel in foreign war theaters. Although the Internet has all but replaced this need, governments worldwide still maintain spectrum protection for radio operators and long distance radio as a kind of backup service.

But as with many selfless deeds and volunteer efforts, those years of giving and standing guard for public communication emergencies have all but been forgotten. Today, most neighborhoods have banned amateurs from constructing effective radio antennas. Such is a bizarre kind of gratitude: *Thank you! We remember what you did for us, but no antennas are allowed.*

Sadly, this seems to be not unlike the dubious need to continuously remind new generations of the efforts of veterans that protected their freedoms. But when *it* hits the proverbial fan, guess who steps up to risk their own safety and to put their lives on the same table as the HOA rules against them? The presence and security factor of Amateur Radio antennas always stands in waiting to protect even those who resent them. Such is not unlike a kind of National Guard - a port in a storm, typically unimportant, until.... [A reprint as a reminder follows.]

SUMMER'S MEMORY

Radio antennas like the one above once graced many an American neighborhood. Then they were a symbol of freedom, and stood as sentries when radio amateurs were called upon to assist in emergencies. Today, they are banned in most residential neighborhoods, and enthusiasts must resort to stealth, nearly invisible, and less efficient arrays. Another lost freedom, yet hams continue to provide communication during satellite and Internet failures even to those who resent their presence. Reading the [Hurricane] "Katrina Files," one becomes starkly aware of the amateur service, and of lives that were saved when conventional communication failed.

*Photos courtesy of "*For all too soon*"*

RICHARD E. TAESCH

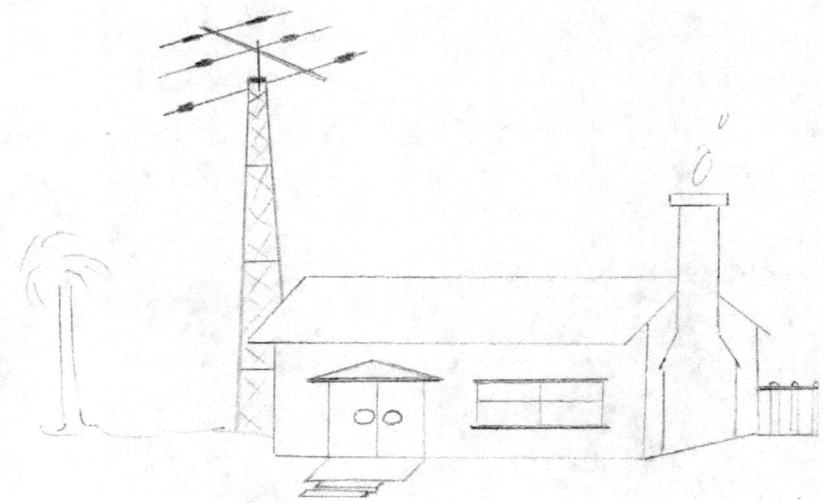

Photos courtesy of "For all too soon"

XIX

How to fail at business and still celebrate life

The "Mr. Tish"* chronicles

Now that you've all been introduced to the "professor" *Tish* (professor title: honorary, of course) throughout these writings, hopefully you have detected a glimpse of humor (here and there) regarding his philosophy on the human predicament.

There is a tune in the Great American Song Book composed by Matt Dennis called *Everything Happens to Me*. (Google the title and look for the *Old Blue Eyes* version - Sinatra.) In short, when most of your business or personal types of interaction either fails or seems to only benefit the other guy (or gal), simply shrug a shoulder, add a smile to the outcome, and leave the conclusion up to interpretation.

It has been said that Walt Disney was once fired from a journalist position because he "lacked imagination!" He then later filed bankruptcies before opening Disneyland. Conversely, such positive outcomes rarely resemble that of Richard's, as he would often end up standing alone following a *deal*, while scratching his head and wondering what happened. A few examples follow.

Mr. "Tish" is a playful name that my friend, Robb, tagged me with. It represents the way some of my students tended to pronounce my last name.

We got 'em - right where they want us

In about 2010, I bought a residential lot at Salton Sea Beach, as it appeared that the community within which my mobile home resides now might close. Calling upon some skills gained in my experimental time in real estate, I researched the property diligently and provided comparable pricing to the seller. Feeling confident in my offer, I drained my savings then presented the offer to him. I proceeded on my own without the aid of a representing broker - an approach that I admonished others to never do. But alas, I *knew what I was doing*, right? Well, maybe not; out comes the familiar head scratching once again.

Unbeknownst to me at first, the seller was a broker and *gladly* accepted my offer "as is." Hmmm! What I didn't know was that the cabin on the lot would soon be condemned by county inspectors and required to be demolished. Years beyond and many fees later would then be needed before I could ever consider living there. Sigh!

To pour water on a drowning man, I could have bought the lot and dwelling across the street in move-in condition for at least a total of $10,000 less, and moved in immediately. I did research that one, but could never find the owners.

Had I been able to move there at that time, I would have saved at least $130,000 in rising lot rent where I still live 11 years later. Well, my neighbor Dennis sure likes his place across the street from my empty lot.

Mr. Tish, the 'un-salesman,' rides again

Following my divorce as described in *For all too soon*, I moved into a duplex in the neighborhood near where I grew up. After a fashion, I decided that I would sell one of my guitars as it was no longer in use. It was an original owner from 1958, then about 25 years old. I had bought it new and financed it with the help of my folks.

A person that I knew and could trust came to me and made the offer of $700 on behalf of an old gentleman who had always wanted one exactly like it. I knew that it was worth more, but felt generous and wanted to make someone happy. I must say that, I've never known a real salesman who ever succeeded that way! Perhaps I instinctively resisted such an occupational identity. Nevertheless, the sale was made and the funds were applied to my estimated taxes. So much for that legacy.

A few months later, I was researching a collector's annual. I then discovered that a one-owner - and unmodified - guitar of the same kind would easily value at about ten times more than what I sold it for. But then again, I did make someone very happy.

Another lost nest egg - going, going, gone

When much younger, one can certainly afford to be *generous (?)* in such ways as I have described thus far. But in the autumn of one's life, not much room is left for such kinds of philanthropy- if I may use that rather colorful term for bad estate planning on my part.

Following the deaths of both my mother and stepdad by 1987, I inherited quite an heirloom in the form of their automobile. It was a 1961 model, brand new the same year I graduated high school. When I took title of the car, its mileage was only ca. 35,000. After I drove it some during times of having no other, it then rested at 64,000 miles for about 30 years in storage. Even then, not including some body work and painting, it would be considered near pristine as all was intact, even the original factory hubcaps. On more than one occasion while visiting a gas station, folks would sometimes approach and offer to buy the car on the spot! Most offers exceeded ten thousand dollars regardless of the faded and peeling paint.

When I bought my home here on 34th Street, my friend and realtor said to me: "Richard, one day that car will be your retirement." As such, in her search for my home as she found it in 1990, she put a very high priority on a safe and covered carport for my treasure to come to rest until one day it might fulfill that legacy.

Time passed, and the things that I would need to do to place it back on the road so as to realize its classic worth became prohibitive.

Even periodic purchase of gasoline just to start the engine was costing hundreds of dollars per year. As such, I agreed to sell it to someone that I knew who understood the history and sentiment of the car.

After viewing it, he carefully asked: "OK; so what do you want for it?"

"Well, the truth is, I don't know. I trust your judgment. Do some research and bring me an offer that you feel is right and fair."

Much time went by as he had personal matters to tend to. I assured him that it would still be here waiting when he was ready. Several more months went by and I was surprised to hear from him. Following a few email exchanges, he made an offer that he felt - considering restoration costs - he could afford.

Initially, I was very disappointed. Well knowing that some collectors were asking well into the high thousands fully restored, I at least thought that perhaps in the $2,000 bracket was something I might expect and was prepared to agree to that. The offer was made at $750!

I stalled for some time, reminding him that the car was one of a kind and it was sentiment to me, etc. He did not respond. Two weeks later I wrote and accepted his offer. Having not had income other than SSA since one year before, the money was now gone, as it covered some living costs and to pay my tax accountant. One might begin to wonder if there was a pattern here. Much the same fate and sale price surrounded my 1958 guitar. That went to pay taxes too.

The buyer was a meaningful long time friend to someone that I also care about. He is now most likely quite happy with his 1961 classic, and that matters to me. Thanks, Charles! You matter too!

I must admit, however, that I am running out of heirlooms to give away

Reprint follows, edited slightly - with a new purpose for my autumn season

The endangered desert turtle cares

In 1970, my wife and I bought five-acres of desert land in hopes for a one-day investment return. The land became part of our divorce settlement, so I held it myself for over thirty years. The predictions for growth in that area never came to be, which is just as well for me. (Hmmm...; I wonder why *that* kinda' rhymes).

As time progressed, my attitudes about business investing and careless development changed. I made a pact with myself that I would donate the land to a nature conservancy before I would ever sell it – even for a profit – to a developer. Offers come to me several times a year, but I consistently refused to respond to them. An official county dirt road crosses the property. It is indeed a strategic location for certain purposes.

Very unexpectedly, a non-profit organization called the *Transition Habitat Conservancy* (THC) contacted me in hopes that I would sell the land to them. The organization strives to purchase and preserve sensitive ecosystems for the protection of wildlife migration routes and transition. Although very pleased that my land would now lie in a conservation area, I was quite emotionally attached to it. I had hoped to one day perhaps visit there for campouts and such. THC offered more for the land than anyone else had, even though it was a fraction of what my wife and I had paid for it. The offer was about $2,500. I agreed to sell the land to them, and few decisions have ever brought such a smile to my face each and every time I think of it.

Conclusion and summary

Now, no tears or pity are required, as Richard has become very comfortable with the conclusion that he is a lousy businessman. And frankly, he's damned proud of it!

Epilogue - and a Dedication

Dear Readers: The previous few pages are not at all about me alone. They are meant as a tribute to the many wonderful folks who have given so much, and shared of themselves to have made my life, and that of others, so meaningful. Such remains an ongoing reminder to just simply give back wherever you can and whenever you can.

" *Just do the work, and the rest will take care of itself.* "
 - Dr. Ernest M. Burgess

XX

Remembrances nearly forgotten

Hopefully autumn will still be with me for a while, as some old stories and life adventures have a way of hiding until our later years. As told about earlier, I tend to discover many of them in *the back country of my mind.* Such are like forgotten trails that have been grown over with brush and trees. Their trail-markers have become somewhat faded and in need of mental restoration.

The first story that follows was probably hidden amongst the proverbial undergrowth of some tangled, and perhaps not so pleasant, memories. Nonetheless, no one's life is ever just about one of us, as all of the actors in a play contribute to the story.

Outtakes from forgotten back trails

In 1976, my cousin from France and her co-traveler, Benoit, came to visit my wife and me for two weeks. One memorable motor home trip provided to them by my mom-in-law and her husband was that of Sequoia National Park.

Throughout the trip, cousin and friend sat rather silently while showing little or no emotion to the magnificent sights of the giant redwoods and other features that they had never witnessed in their young lives before.

This began to aggravate mom-in-law. She was beginning to feel that they simply had little or no appreciation for the special effort and expense that she and her husband had put forth. As an observer, I withheld my comments or opinion, but gave the situation much thought over a few days time. At the right moment, I sat down next to Evelyne and Benoit and asked if I could ask them a personal question about our family in France.

"Of course." Evelyne replied.

"Evelyne, you may remember that my father, your uncle Edmund, made his last trip to France to see your grandparents and other family."

"Yes; my mother spoke of it often. Why do you ask?"

"Well, I was very small then. But I do seem to remember that my dad expressed to my mother that he felt his oldest brother, Charles, your uncle also, seemed very cold and non-expressive to him when he made that trip."

"No, I don't remember that part as I never met my Uncle Edmund."

"Evelyne, the reason I brought it up is that it might be since my father had been in the U.S. for a long time, perhaps he had just become somewhat *Americanized*. I've often wondered if he had simply forgotten about the French ways that his brother Charles still had."

Intuitively knowing exactly why I had brought this up, she smiled warmly and replied: "Of course! Your mother-in-law must surely think that we have no emotion or gratitude to seeing these beautiful things that they have brought us to enjoy."

"How did you guess?"

"Well you see, when you Americans see something unusual for the first time such as a giant tree, you often exhibit emotion, loudness, and excitement. We, on the other hand, may just be overwhelmed. We internalize the same excitement, but may not show it as you do."

"I thought as much, Evelyne, but I just wanted to be sure. Once and for all, I needed to try and understand that story about my father and Uncle Charles."

I did attempt to explain my revelations to mom, but perhaps out of conditioning of some kind, she made no comment.

* * *

Although now only making private flights, the retired Air Force pilot loved to take pleasure trips with his new wife. He owned a four-passenger Beechcraft Bonanza in partnership along with two other compatible associates. The group owners would take turns at different times which worked out quite well.

On this trip while traveling south along the Baja peninsula coastline, John and Mary became aware of a storm brewing and visibility becoming quite difficult. They descended low so as to spot a viable landing option on the hard sand of the beach. They soon noticed a section where there appeared to be several other private planes that had also landed for the duration of the storm.

For their landing, John picked a flat spot that seemed to be quite a distance from the others. Most were camping in a kind of group, building warm fires and making meals.

"John," exclaims Mary, "why don't we just taxi over there and join them? It might be fun to make a kind of family gathering out of this."

"No, Mary, I think it best to settle here. We can always walk over there and visit no matter." Mary, not being a pilot herself, submitted to John's instincts as he was usually right about such things. She was puzzled, but did not argue further.

Morning came, and it was a beautiful sunny day just right for flying on to continue their trip. Oddly enough, the tide had come in during the night and completely surrounded the other planes now marooned on the high spot that they had all gathered on. It had become a kind of temporary island that was impossible to navigate any kind of takeoff, at least until low tide later that day.

John winks at Mary, as they were quite able to take off. While slowly becoming airborne, both warmly waved at the others. All stood and looked up in a kind of: "Oh well, we just thought that they were being anti-social."

* * *

One bandleader that we often worked for would sometimes travel out of town on business either for the American Legion or certain law enforcement gatherings. Jay was a retired policeman, but still led the police band and booked gigs for his own dance bands as well.

Our trumpet player had a wonderful sense of humor, and often came up with the most entertaining capers. It just happened to be that he and his wife were going to be in the same city and hotel on a vacation that Jay was scheduled to be staying at on business. While planning their trip, trumpet player packs his black gig suit and trumpet armed with a plan.

Scenario: Both Jay and horn player are far across country from where they live. Trumpet man dons his gig suit, carries his trumpet in its case, and locates Jay's room. Jay happened to be engaged in a poker game. Trumpet knocks on the door; Jay opens it and stares in disbelief while horn man - looking down at his watch - recites:

"Hey Jay! What time did you say the gig here tonight was?"

* * *

Our trumpet man, Russ, had a notorious reputation for always making the gig on time, but just barely. He'd often be pulling his horn out of the case just moments before Jay would count the first dance tune off.

This particular night was a booking at the very prestigious Hilton hotel. It was the grand banquet dinner dance for a national convention of law-enforcement agencies. The ensemble was a reduced big band - four horn front line, bass, piano, drums, and yours truly on guitar. The starting time was nigh. Jay was understandably pissed, as Russ still had not shown up. This was not good because the kick-off arrangement was a fanfare and required a trumpet solo for the opening part.

'Damn it all, that a-hole is gonna' be late this time, and of all the damn nights! Screw him; we're going to start anyway. Richard, cover his part, PLEASE!"

"But Jay, it's in a trumpet key."

"Well then, damn it, transpose it! Uh one - Uh two - three - four ..."

As I rubbernecked across to see the horn book to be the hero, the intro starts! Lo and behold, we hear the trumpet part being played far across the room, but from where no one could tell.

Here comes Russ walking through the grand doors of the ballroom. He was making his way politely through the crowd: horn in right hand with fingers on the valves, his case in the left hand, while playing the part perfectly and saving my proverbial rear end.

Conclusion: Russ was able to uphold his reputation of always making it by the seat of his pants. Try as he might to be pissed, Jay was near doubled over in laughter while still trying to play drums to back the band. "Next tune:"

"OK guys," calls Jay, "get up number 75: *I didn't Know What Time it Was.*"

***

Perhaps I should have dedicated a full chapter on the many students that provided me with delightful laughter - the kind that keeps one smiling indefinitely and loving his job.

Stanly, just six-years old, and Eric at thirteen, were not unlike a comedy team such as Abbot and Costello without ever knowing it. They were wonderful Pilipino boys, and both active in my children's classic guitar ensemble at that time.

I was just out of sight of our director, but able to hear the boys current conversation in the waiting room following one of our rehearsals. Stanly had been struggling with a passage in the third guitar part. He was now looking for some comfort from his mischievous older brother. Following, is the conversation as I remember it:

"Hey Eric, what did you think this time.?"
"Of what?" he annoyingly blasts back.
"You know, of that part I always mess up; was it OK?"
"Well, ... If you ask me, it sounded like a fart!"

Meanwhile, having heard this delightful exchange, I was about to lose it in laughter from the next room. While peeking in at them unnoticed, there's Stanly - with eyes closed tight - laughing convulsively, and even harder than I was.

Out the door of her office storms the director who thought she heard what she did. She beckons for me, and angrily declares in a stern, righteous way: "Richard, Richard! Did I just hear what I think I heard from those two idiots?"

"Sorry Miss B, I was not listening at that moment; must have been concentrating on my next class." mumble I, while trying to keep a straight face.

* * *

The man with 1,000 yachts, one airplane, and lots-a' kids

Our motor home adventure heading towards the very southern end of Baja California, began near the north end of the *Sea of Cortez* (Gulf of California). The sea is not far below the northern border of Mexico. A forty-five minute diversion off of the main highway #1, took us to a very sparsely populated old seaport called L.A. Bay - otherwise known as *Bahia de Los Angeles* in Spanish.

As our driver, Jim, slowly approached the settlement by dirt road, I couldn't help but to notice a very curious collection of what appeared to be small abandoned and deteriorating yachts spread about. Some were half in water, others were still moored, and some scattered about the shore as in a kind of ghost town scene. None looked all that seaworthy, but then Richard is rather unfamiliar with such things at best. Sunbathers and sailors were nowhere in sight. As I glanced to my right, other than small children playing about, my eyes gravitated to the light Cessna aircraft parked at the end of a short make-do kind of airstrip.

Jim knew the history of Baja quite well, and loved to share stories of his many trips there, some even in his own plane. As we slowly came to rest in the shade of several tropical trees, a great and peaceful silence engulfed our presence while we took in all that mystified us. No one spoke, or asked what would be typically expected at such a magical moment. After a few minutes of what seemed more like a group of monks in meditation, Jim smiled warmly and began his tale.

As history tells it, *Papa Diago* - the village owner and tribal chief of a few generations - had apparently fathered most of the children we saw running about. He was also the pilot of the Cessna, and now owner of the many subject yachts.

"Hmmmm, Jim," I stuttered, "but why...., when, and just how did all of this come about?"

If I were to describe any such moment resulting in a speechless pall that seemed to be gripping us, this was clearly it.

Chuckling somewhat mischievously, Jim continues [paraphrased]:

"As I understand it, many folks over time have tried to venture here in their boats, not unlike the many you see scattered about. Boat or plane was just about the only way for visitors to come before the new highway was built. They would leave coastal ports near Los Angeles then begin the long sailing trip south all the way to Cabo San Lucas, which is at the tip of Baja. They would round the cape then sail north in the gulf until they came to this area. The trip took perhaps weeks or even months to complete.

"Once they arrived and vacationed here, they would realize that if they left for the trip back at that time, weather changes and post summer storms would make the sea journey treacherous, if not impossible. The only safe way would be to wait here at least a year before attempting to sail home."

"Could they do that?" I queried, "and how would they maintain themselves for that long in such a place? What about their jobs?"

"Well," continues Jim: "enters our *Papa Diago*. Senior Diago would offer the *kind* and *humanitarian* proposition that, if they gave him the boats that they came in, he would gladly fly them home in said airplane. Such was not more than an hour or so away by air. Since the only option was the one I mentioned, they would jump at the opportunity. Thus the collage of old boats, many of which our smiling businessman would then sell to others for income. Si?"

XXI

Little joys

VIGNETTES

The Buffalo

Victoria and I would often take early morning walks to the back fields of the William S. Hart Park near her home. Walking down a little dirt road beyond apartment buildings would take us to the fenced boundary. Behind the fence several large bison and their little calves were kept as part of the park attractions.

One couldn't help but to notice that this out of the way route was used by trucks to deliver hay for daily feeding of the animals within. The trucks would somehow lift loads of the feed over the fence to be consumed by the buffalo and their kids. As we ventured past following their breakfast or dinner time, the food would be completely gone as expected. However, a considerable amount of hay that had fallen from the delivery truck always remained outside of the fence.

We soon noticed that when anyone would walk into view of the animals, they would begin slowly and cautiously to move from afar and come towards us. "How interesting," we thought. It soon became apparent that others must have begun a familiar pageant of picking up the hay scraps and holding pieces through openings in the fence. Such became a welcome source of extra snacks for the buffalo.

Later in the season, most of the tourists who made the discovery were now gone. As my companion and I took up the watch alone, we gained much joy holding the food and letting the creatures take it from our hands. It soon became quite a regular event. Even if the little families were an acre or two beyond the fence, as soon as they spotted us they would begin to migrate towards, recognizing both of us in anticipation and without fear. Trivia, sure! But *little joys* are never *little* to that child within us.

Horseradish?

"Excuse me, sir! Would you happen to know where they might keep the ice picks here?" asked the rather confused-looking man as I searched over the shelves for something that I needed.

He was an elderly man, but looked quite well-kept and sturdy. His groomed white hair and turned up mustache gave to a friendly and thoughtful kind of fellow, as was his demeanor. Somehow there was a kind of "old friend" air about him.

I answered him as I kept looking: "Good question! I'm not having much luck either."

"I've been looking everywhere, and it seems that no one has even heard of such a thing." He commented.

"Well, trying to find an ice pick here might be like looking for horseradish in the *Aldi* food market" I responded.

"Oh my," he fired back, "there is a horseradish called *"Atomic Horseradish"* at the .... Market ..."

Before he could even finish his joy of furnishing me with his discovery, I immediately turned as we gazed face to face like two little kids in a toy store. "Yes, yes! I know that one, and it is God's answer to horseradish! None like it anywhere."

At that point we expanded on the virtues of our common love for the item, and seemed to have both forgotten about what we came into the store for to begin with.

"Why don't you try to make an ice pick out of a long and large nail?" I offered. "You can make up a simple wooden handle for it, and I'll bet it will work!"

"Of course! I never thought of that; that would be easy."

Off we both went on our separate ninety-nine-cent store shopping safaris, smiling ear to ear, both with warm feelings of camaraderie with our fellow man. Come to think of it, we never shook hands or gave names - just having too much joy in the moment for things that are much more important.

Honk if you love Jesus

Traffic was typically slow and annoying as Jason pulled up behind the car in front of him at the stoplight. It seemed like every street had a stop and every driver was in a sweat and in a hurry.

With gritting of teeth and angst, he suddenly spots a lovely bumper sticker on the car in front of him with the saying: *Honk if you love Jesus!* With a warm and renewed spirit, Jason follows the invitation and honks his car horn. The fellow pauses rather long before proceeding on the now green light. Without hesitation, the driver lurches ahead with an angry waving arm from his window, bearing the venerable *California Salute* in return.

With a deep sigh of disappointment in humanity, Jason remembers the title of a song by Michael Franks: "Sometimes I Just Forget to Smile."

Why don't you just....

While having a telephone consultation with the music Professor, Dr. Long, we discussed a blind student that I had prepared for the university music department. She proceeded to ask a very logical question:

"Richard, I know that Julie is writing her melodic dictation quiz in braille while the others do it in print notation; but since I don't know anything about braille, how can I be sure that she is doing it correctly?"

"Well, Dr. Long, why don't you just ask her to read it back to you?"

"Oh my," she quietly and humbly responds: "I never thought of that."

> *The following joy belongs exclusively to me and the little ecologist in the story. It is a reprint, but quite appropriate to qualify as a Little Joy here!* [R.T.]

Family Ties

Hiking along a rather popular trailhead for families and children, a mom and her little boy were just slightly in front of my companion and me. The little fellow was no more than waist high – close enough to the ground for spotting litter along the way.

Unaware of anyone observing him, he would often bend down to pick up the careless leftovers, while seemingly quite proud of his contribution to our planet.

"Jimmy, stop that! You can't be picking up every piece of trash you see; please behave yourself, or we'll go back to the car!" exclaims mom in annoyance.

Obviously quite hurt and near tears, he turns to see if anyone might have witnessed his humiliating chastising. I smile ever so warmly directly at him, wink, and give a hearty *thumbs up!* Knowing quite well why, he peeks up at mom to make sure she's not watching, smiles wonderfully at me, and hides his own thumbs-up response to us behind her back.

Cute? Sure, perhaps; but ...

The little beggar of Scotty's Castle

Several motor homes were lined up along with our own, all setting up camp so as to be early the next morning for the castle tour in Death Valley, California.

It is said that the coyote is the most intelligent of all canines. Over time, one little fellow had certainly used his smarts to gain the affection of the tourists among campers.

Watching a wild predator sitting patiently and waiting at each motor home door for a hand out, was just too much fun for the touring folks to resist. Door to door he would go, not unlike children doing Trick or Treat on Halloween. Some of the regulars who probably came each year hoping to visit the "visitor," would enjoy watching "Wiley" take the bread directly from their hands. He would then move to the next *soft touch* for another treat. Yes, we all know it's a no-no to feed wildlife. But by this time, the celebrity entertainer had been so spoiled by the event that ... oh well!

Scotty's Castle, Death Valley, California

XXII

My world in autumn

Our last chapter, 24, will be a kind of epilogue for the last adventure in a long career in music - since 1961. It will be in the form of the well-published article that began my work in music literacy for the blind in 1994. Its purpose and mission still applies in 2022. As said earlier, it will be a full circle statement of commitment on behalf of those who have come before. Although soon approaching thirty years since publication, such has become a chronicle. The principles of freedom through literacy and independence for the blind or sighted in any endeavor, are never outdated.

Preparing the setting for Chapter 24, the chapter *Little Joys* sought to reach out to the heart of the child in us. A child whose curiosity and appreciation for the *little things,* prepares the spirit for impossible dreams and final missions - and who knows, perhaps even beyond.

Of all the progress and accomplishments of those who have made history in this work, none speaks louder than the fact that the literacy movement never needs updating in its goal. The challenges in a materialistic world will always be there and remain an uphill effort. But they will never be less than motivating to those who persevere - and who *just do the work.*

* * *

The literacy movement treatise is a classic example of combining what I call "a harmony of opposites." Never before as in 2022, have I become more acutely aware that, if we disagree, we are sometimes thought to be "divided." Perhaps we even feel somewhat at war with someone that we disagree with. We blame the concept of that which we disagree with as being negative. Or perhaps, a better way to say it is: the differing view is a culprit that divides friends and / or family due to strong sentiments on anything from politics, to religion, to morals and ethics. We thereby attribute guilt to the opposite side. "You're wrong, and I am right" seems to govern the arguments.

In Richard's mind, more and more he seems to observe a positive pattern in that, when folks have opposite views, those opposing energies really want to see the same outcome. For example, whether you bend *right* or *left* politically, in the long-term time frame one only wants to see who he or she believes is best for the gig. The approach may differ, and private interests are notwithstanding. But what we believe, so shall it be in either of our collective *point and view.*

Why then is it so terrible for us to be divided? I have observed many friends or associates that have - at one time or another - cited the opposite view on world affairs as "turning us against each another." To me the differences are what enable a safe balance and not at all destructive. And most of all, to be in the minority in the way one views a trend should never become something to be ashamed of. Mark Twain is known to have expressed that - paraphrased: *when one finds oneself on the side of the majority, it may be time to pause and to reflect.* We must always remember that a large factor leading to WWII was that one side wanted the world to believe only what they thought was right. Compromise was not acceptable until the damage was already done.

In my 1994 article, for example, the controversy of those who insist that the blind should learn music by ear only, vs. those who feel that reading from the beginning is best, has a common and very compatible principal. Simply that, the "harmony of opposites" can be applied so as to hear with the eye or braille touch senses, and to see with the ear. One cannot be separated from the other if either is to survive in a sighted world.

At one time, a majority of teachers felt that ear-only was best. So then who was right - the majority or the minority, and which seemed to endure over time? Who is to define which side is best, other than to harmonize both resources? So to *pause and reflect* might be worth considering for that underlying desire of all to want the same thing - that is a positive result. I'll respect your way of thinking, if you will respect mine!

***

SHORT STORIES - Points & Views #8
Beethoven's dilemma

As the workshop began, I observed many faces of the blind young adults in attendance as seeming to be quite suspicious of this stranger coming to lecture them on why they should consider learning to read music.

A demonstration called *The Seven Little Steps to Read Music in Braille* did seem to bring on some giggling and joy. The ear-only musicians found that within about twenty minutes, they were actually reading music! First, we used numbers in braille, then turned them into music braille notes. I divided the class into groups of two, and three parts for singing in ensembles. Well, *Mary Had a Little Jam* was a huge success, and there were even some comments like: *Hey! I can do this. Wow!* So a couple of jokes later, I was in the club, so to speak.

Soon, a rather skeptical-appearing young lady held her hand up so as to ask a question. "Yes; would you like to ask something?" I remarked.

"Yes, thank you. Why would I want to go into depth and the time it takes to learn to read when I've been playing by ear for years?"

"Thank you, young lady, as that is a very fine question. Now to answer that, let me ask one of you."

"Like?"

"Like, how many recorded versions do you think there are of Beethoven's *Pathetique* Sonata?"

"Oh, I've played that."

"Surely; but how many versions from different editions do you think have been recorded over time?"

"Uh, well, maybe at least several hundred."

'OK! Which version would you recommend that a student copy by ear, and how do you know that it is the best one? "

After a long hesitation: "I think I see what you mean."

"And, could you be sure that it was an *Urtext* version?"

"An *Ur*... what?"

"Well, that is what some feel to be the most reliable manuscript representing the composer's own hand."

"(Sigh) Guess I better learn to at least read some things in the music braille code after all; especially since I want to teach."

> The following story might well be thought of as based on a philosophy. Perhaps more specifically described, it is a true story resulting from a startling discovery, followed sometime later by a discussion between the author and a dear friend. It is a perfect example of two differing philosophies, divided economic backgrounds, and perhaps one recent rethinking regarding certain personal leanings. Notice the air of flexibility and compromise without loss of conviction - a true contrast to that described in another discussion about divided opinions earlier in this chapter.

Just a paycheck away

I was driving with a friend on a specific shopping day safari. Our destination was in a rather industrial neighborhood not far from where I grew up and later taught in a school. As we exited the freeway and descended the familiar off-ramp just as I had done for many years, I was amazed at what appeared to be much trash and litter on the green landscape along the sides.

"Walter, what in the world is this? It was never littered before. Where did it all come from?"

"Com-on', Richard, you certainly must know that there's a homeless crisis in California?" [2022]

"Well, yeah, ... uh, but what does this have to do with it?"

"Didn't you see the tents and make-shift shelters scattered around? These areas have become encampments where many folks who cannot afford, or have been put out of their homes and apartments, take up residence trying to survive."

The mess and massive impact of this discovery was overwhelming, to say the very least. I'd heard of, and was quite aware of homelessness, but never witnessed it to such an extent before.

As the day went on, we chatted some about it. Following our mission, we proceeded to drive back heading north on old San Fernando Road towards our home. On my right as a passenger, as far ahead as I could see were old rundown-looking motor homes parked. There were also trailers - usually with a pickup truck, hood up, and a tattered fellow trying to fix it. All appeared moored along the side somewhat permanently. There seemed to be no end to the miles and miles of what must have become a kind of temporary mobile homeless encampment. Following, is the discussion as described in the prologue above.

Alan remarks: "I just don't have any empathy for most of these so-called *homeless*. Since Covid, the work force is short of workers and employers are begging for help. I think that these people just don't want to work."

"Well, Alan, I can't help but think that not all of them feel that way." I then described what I had seen, and another situation where a long time tenant who also lived in my own community had to walk away from his home and live in a van.

"You're probably right, Richard, but having been in retail work and owning a business, I guess it's hard for me to understand.

'Sure, I can see how you'd feel that way. Face it, Al, you and I grew up in a much different California. Even at my age now, I cannot believe what it has become.

"I guess so."

"Alan, look at it this way: the average one-bedroom apartment rent these days is near $2,500 in L.A. County [2022]. Do the math! One has to earn a minimum of $30,000 per year just to cover base rent alone here, not including utilities, food, medical, kids, and whatever.

"So; things are tough."

"Alan, how many folks do you know, including your own kids, could handle that if they had not already been established, or perhaps just moved here with nothing and following hard times?"

"I guess that could be *any of us.*"

"Yes, and best remember that most people who are not retired may be just a paycheck away from the same fate. Alan, no one wants to live that way."

> A warning sign placed on some trash containers - L.A. County - displays a photo of handcuffs. The caption reads:
>
> Scavenging is stealing and punishable by law!
>
> Why is that? Hoovervilles 2000, perhaps?

Escape with me now to ponder a vision:

They came, and they came, and they came to pursue their California Dream - and they continue to come, not unlike the migrant farm workers during the Great Depression. With one-way tickets, they come by plane; they come by motor home, car, or just in their dreams. They come for the weather, for hope, for a new chance - a new chance to make the valleys, the deserts, the mountains and the seashore their final destiny.

Many are unaware of the reality that they are entering what has become perhaps one of the most expensive places in the nation within which to survive. Not until they arrive and all resources have been exhausted to explore the dream, do most realize that it's one way only. For many families, there may be no choice to go back. They line grass mediums with tents in affluent communities, they park worn out motor homes along the byways, under freeway bridges, and sleep in flood control channels.

Once migrants arrive to the Golden State, they only find a worsening situation as rental housing has become well beyond the means of even many native Californians. Sure there is work available, lots of it. But most will never earn enough to afford decent housing. Even rental property owners themselves are strapped with unmanageable maintenance costs. It is unlikely that there will ever be a way to bring rental fees into a reality for most without government relief.

I have learned that the Depression migrants were those who tried to flee from their lost homes and farming livelihoods caused by the drought-ravaged Midwest. They were often lured to California by colorful brochures and invitations to a better life with abundant work and fine working conditions. The crop growers promised nirvana, but once here, the families only found the same hopelessness from which they had fled. They arrived hoping to find what was once a place of abundance and potential, only to starve and succumb to sickness and poverty.

Outtake

During the Great Depression, *homelessness* as we now see it in modern times, was apparently rather common. Homeless encampments thrived nationally as do now in California. Then, the government resisted providing relief for those displaced from their homes by the Depression. Many farm worker migrant families were from the drought-ravaged Dust Bowl. Encampments were called "Hoovervilles," as President Herbert Hoover was largely blamed for the situation.

One very sad story was about a group of (then recent) World War I veterans in 1932. They had been promised by Congress to be paid for their service. Betrayed, they formed an encampment near the capitol in Washington D.C. under protest.

Under a presidential order they were forcefully removed from their camp, which was then burned to the ground. (Source and further details can be found on Internet. Search: **Hoovervilles**.)

Emmy Lou

When I walked into the Marina Village Market and Cafe as I had done many times upon visiting my future home community, I sensed a rather strange and cold energy. Emmy Lou had been the owner and proprietor of Beach Marina since perhaps the early sixties when I first discovered the seaside oasis and cantina. Although we never chatted much, she was always friendly and usually smiling in a welcoming way. As I approached the counter this day, she didn't seem very anxious to look up or to speak. She simply continued looking down at her knitting needles while she worked on a blanket-type of item. She seemed to be escaping from some kind of reality unknown to me.

Beach Marina was always an interesting icon on the west shore. Its history goes back to a tiny store for boaters and campers to purchase supplies for their boating, skiing, and fishing vacations. I always enjoyed telling of the times that, when one would enter the store, he or she would routinely bend down as the floor was constantly being raised with boards. You see, the water level in the desert sea continued to rise. As a temporary fix to postpone rebuilding the place, one simply became accustomed to shopping while bent over somewhat. This was due to the fact that the little building was set on the same water level as the launching inlets.

Eventually, the building was replaced by a very lovely facility. Although now without the fun of coping with the rising tide, it was somewhat of an iconic disappointment for us adventuresome regulars. The new marina was quite sophisticated, complete with an outdoor wooden deck right over the water inlet. One could watch boats come and go while dining at lunch and enjoying a spectacular view. Boaters would navigate past you while lining up at the private fuel station - a welcomed part of marina services.

But today, I couldn't help but to wonder at the fact that there appeared to be no customers anywhere in sight, nor any sign of boaters bustling near the launches.

Although I sensed that changes were in the future for the area, what was once a popular and lively water sports attraction now seemed to be a kind of ghost village. Even the campsites on the beach were deserted. It had been some time since I had visited there, as my moving plans had been delayed for quite a while.

I glanced over to Emmy Lou still knitting away, and mentioned that the water level in the little bays seemed low. She nodded, glanced up smiling weakly and said, "Richard, walk over and take a look at our bulletin board." I complied, and there - posted in official notice - was the unspeakable: *'All camping at this west shore beach will be terminated as of .... Recreational activities are no longer permitted according to county authority regulations.'*

How could this be? Generations of seaside recreation at perhaps one of the highest visited water facilities in the state now just ends - no explanation, just gone! And yes, my own home for one day is only yards away from the marina.

Well, apparently, Hurricane Katherine having struck the Gulf of California in the late 70's, also took quite a toll on this area, most of which never recovered. Now I could see the reason the shores were receded, and that mitigation efforts would now be necessary so as to prevent further erosion. Efforts to continue inflow have stopped, sea birds die daily, and the smell of dying fish on shorelines is ever present. [Could perhaps this have something to do with recent discoveries of rich lithium sources beneath the sea?]

The marina was soon closed and the building condemned. Broken hearted, Emmy Lou passed away just a short time after. Inactivity and neglect has left the largest body of water in California - some 400 square miles in size - inhabited by ghost towns and a kind of sub-society of migrant farm workers. They are now living in what has become the poorest of counties in the entire state. What was once called the "California Riviera" - bountiful in abundance and potential - is no more.

Worst of all, many Californians do not know that such a place existed, its history, nor that even Santa Claus once visited the children of family campers on its beaches every December. On cue, he would water ski into bays towed by a ski boat sporting a Christmas tree on its bow. Dressed in a red and white wetsuit, he would release, then ski up onto the beach bringing little gifts to happy kids camping with families away from their homes on Christmas.

And if the wound is not deep enough, residents living on the southeast shores endure dust storms from exposed playa. This often causes children to end up in hospitals with serious lung disorders. And so goes the story of another lost paradise, and political priorities with different plans and different *points of view.**

See Saving the Salton Sea - *a 2013 documentary video found on YouTube.*

XXIII

Autumn's parting thoughts

    Richard tends to listen to the news as seldom as possible, but does catch the highlights a few times a week while shaving.

    After my music session this morning - Veteran's Day, 2021 - the news featured a story about what some call *global warming*. The story indicated that it is accelerating faster now than it has for thousands of years. This seemed quite timely, as I had been jotting down notes for a rather serious chapter from a late-in-life viewpoint before closing *Summer's Memory*.

    My own thought on the subject is not important, other than that climate change has been with us since the beginning of time. Clearly, civilization must have some impact on acceleration. However, opportunists do prefer to keep us stirred up for their own purposes, and this one is no exception. As said, Richard's opinion is his own. Although not particularly relevant, sobering thoughts about today's attitudes on environment - or man's ignoring of it - do once again stir this teacher's instincts - if only that of a simple observer of trending concerns.

    Yes, like the retired typewriter repairman in an earlier chapter, I do lean a bit towards the sentiment that: "... folks wake up, as we're simply going the wrong way!" I truly believe that no LED light bulb, hybrid, or electric car is going to ever fix what is wrong. It's simply up to us - the consumer and the people - to finally grasp the unpopular concept of what we can do without. Sadly, such will never fly. We hypocritically promote the gospel of conserving energy, while at the same time continue to expand the economic benefits and systems to meet an ever increasing and insatiable demand. The demand will never slow! Face that, and the former message might seem to have some merit. Perhaps it may even become the primary answer to our very survival on this planet.

Offering conservation rebates only to goad customers into spending more money on purchasing (e.g. water-saving) devices won't cut it either. We must see that these are only deceptive marketing strategies. Such are intended to sell, promote, and otherwise nudge us, while evading the same facts that convince us to consume more. We simply continue to waste rather than to help ourselves and our future generations. Who then will set examples of lasting wisdom and independence?

No one seems willing to give up their constant updating and more powerful devices. Technology will never fix this problem. As the cynic's definition of *technology* in Chapter 10 warns: Technology is *a science commonly valued beyond, or in preference to, its benefits.* As often applied in business, it only leads to profit motivation, rarely to solutions for lasting conservation. And the pursuit of profits in the business world as a priority, never seems to end in any way other than that of demise.

Sometimes it may seem that, when we read stirring things such as within books like *Silent Spring* by Rachel Carson, we might feel a responsibility, but helpless to make changes. Not so! Each of us can contribute even though we may not live to see the collective effects. We all contribute to some eco-demise in one way or another, if not just the simple act of living and breathing. So perhaps ask yourself: "just what energy consumptive habit can I live without, or if not, perhaps minimize unnecessary usage?" What is necessary? What is not? And if one should think that it doesn't make a difference, remember this message: *Just do the work,* and watch others take notice! Never, ever try to explain why, as few will ever *quite get it,* nor should it matter. (See Chapter II.)

Before finishing this part of my remembrance, I will leave you with the last series of short stories and outtakes that you have become familiar with. Please view them in light humor as perhaps just fictional fantasies. But do consider them as though they might be possible. Such are based only upon my own observations of human nature. But they are influenced by other thinkers held high in my esteem such as Einstein, Steinbeck, and more.

So perhaps Richard can leave this world one day feeling that he has done his best to contribute some things to ponder. By means of fictional reality in his little stories, maybe, just maybe there might be a glimmer of hope that others will join to turn this "wrong way" around and into a new millennium of healing and wisdom.

SHORT STORIES - Points & Views for the last season #9

Virtual (non) reality

It was a lovely and warm autumn day, and although students were becoming restless and somewhat anxious to begin a long weekend, Professor Clay's class was always one that the college kids enjoyed and put themselves into. Weekend notwithstanding, they were all ears and even put their covert snacks out of sight for his lecture.

"Speaking of ...." as silence and wide eyes focused on Prof. Clay; "Dr. Al [Einstein] was known to have said that his definition of insanity was *doing the same thing over and over again and expecting different results.* Let us ...."

"Dr. Clay," interrupts Melvin, "that just cannot be true in all circumstances. I wonder just what Bro Albert was smoking when he wrote that one?"

"Mel," - Clay patiently indulges the young man as he holds his lecture up - "I too would like to know that, as it must have been some pretty good stuff!" (As the class quietly roars with laughter) "Perhaps you might explain what you mean before we continue with where I, uh, left off *ahhemmmm.*"

"So sorry sir, but since this is a music college, such a statement cannot apply to every situation like old Doc Albert infers. For example, a musician who will practice daily always does the same things over and over and may hope for different results, but not always immediately overcome his or her *c-l-a-m-s*."

"Clams?" queries Clay.

"Yeah! You know; bad notes; we call 'em grace clams. Kinda' like grace notes, but wrong ones. We fix 'em by repeating them and call 'em grace clams."

"Well, Melvin, Al probably learned that from another Stein called Dr. Franken*stein* who gave us his own lesson about messing with Mother Nature. Now can I get on with my lecture?"

"Sure, doc; sorry about that."

Professor Clay gives it another try

"Good afternoon class!" cheerfully states Dr. Clay while launching yet another session in college philosophy 101. "Today we will further discuss the principal of energy conservation vs. that of supply and demand."

Well armed with two classic examples of sharply differing philosophies, Clay opens his lecture with two typical subject characters for illustration. His hope in today's lesson is to demonstrate a principal that will provide an example of bottom line solidarity in favor of its lasting benefit as opposed to short-term economic gains. Of course, the concept is often counterproductive to stock market growth, consequently opposite of the eco-minded.

"How many of you here today have ever heard of John Muir?" As expected, well over half of the class waves arms enthusiastically proud of being so well informed.

"OK! Jerry, can you tell us - in one short sentence - what Mr. Muir brings to mind?"

Jerry hesitates, then convincingly states: "Careful planning to preserve natural resources for future generations."

"Quite astutely stated, Jerry! Now! Those who have heard of the name 'Pinchot' raise hands." Perhaps about five brave warriors venture to make their rather weak showing of hands.

"Well, Jerry, it looks like you're on for the explanation on the Muir side." Jerry stands up sheepishly, clears his throat, and begins:

"John was a strong naturalist who believed that natural resources must be carefully and thoughtfully spent so as to see them last into the future for those to come."

"Brilliant! Myrtle, your hand was up for the Pinchot team; what do you know about him?"

"Thank you, Professor! Gordon Pinchot and Mr. Muir were actually very good friends. Gordon was the first American director of forestry. However, he and John disagreed on their views of conservation in that Pinchot believed that resources should be used freely and only to benefit man's immediate needs and economic stability."

"Not bad, Myrtle; we can use that example just fine for our purpose here today. Now, can you give us a strong case for the beliefs of one of those gentlemen?"

"Well, for starters, there's a famous trail crossing the Sierra Nevada wilderness called the *John Muir Trail*. It has survived as a monument to Muir for many generations."

"OK." responds Professor Clay. "Who would like to tackle any lasting virtues of Mr. Pinchot in the long term benefit arena? In other words, how do you think that he might be remembered by future generations?"

One timid hand slowly raises and offers his side for the effort of the day.

"Well, Dr. Clay, it's really not fair! No one I know here has heard enough about Gordon Pinchot to present a balanced opinion. But for what it may be worth, I remember the two political terms, *hawk; dove.* They represent to me the two kinds of gentleman being discussed here. One is not bad or the other good, and both are creatures to be respected. Yet one will profess either a gentle or a predator type of impression - your choice. But," as he smiles mischievously, "I have heard of a new bird being added to those terms for balance as it were."

"Jerry, do you have a point, or are you becoming a law student?" asks Clay seeming quite puzzled yet very curious." (Class chuckles)

"Yes sir! I, um, ... I believe that the new bird is the *Ostrich!* It is the one that is known to put its head in the sand so as to not be noticed."

* * *

Outtakes

George Oh Well would be proud

> *The following two gems represent two (fictional) talk show broadcasts.*

[Week 1]

Journalist's opening statement: "In depth discussion on some radio and TV shows has become quite well frequented in today's trending and conflicting society. This morning we will explore some typical discussions that have been heard as of late. (The following discussions are transcribed and paraphrased, and do not necessarily reflect the opinions or policy of this station - **WBS**.)"

"*Text message implant devices* are currently being explored for future newborn children. Such devices resemble the venerable Pace Maker for heart patients, but will be implanted at birth not unlike the routine circumcision for male children. [Host's commentary: 'circum ... who? Not my kid you don't'].

"The text device will make it possible for humans to communicate with each other freely as though using Internet phones, but without the phone. A special governor feature will be included for children under 18 so as to prevent the obvious exchanging of test answers between classmates in school.

"The device works on a simple principle thus: A tickle in the lower abdomen signals a notification message waiting to come through. The receptor gently pushes on the belly button and a quiet voice is heard within the inner ear. However, to respond does require a real Internet phone so as to assure the device makers of their yearly updating profits. Welcome to 2084!"

[Week 2 - special virtual Fathers Day edition]

"*Virtual conception* is slowly becoming more of a possibility, not unlike crypto currency which eliminates the need for value-backed purchasing entities.

"Virtual conception is particularly attractive in our trend for Zoom-type of relationships that eliminate the need for masks and traditional, rather complex, human contact and inter ... (oops; can't say that here).

"So many controversial issues will no longer become problematical as we pursue this exciting idea in virtual parenting. Masks during mating will not be required by law, thereby simplifying the act of breathing.

"In essence, once a virtual computer relationship has been established between attracted individuals, a delivery service administered and maintained by *RamaSchlong* Prime Express will provide the receptive party with the merchandise needed to complete the......... (C'mon use your imagination! George did.)

"C'mon dads, they're not called *programs*! They are called *apps* now. Get with it dudes, will ya!

"Until next week, this is *Dan Gasser* bidding you all a goodnight!"

Richard's Epilogue ....
And last (virtual) pedagogical effort - with a wink and a warm smile

As I gaze upon the sheep in flocks following the trends with so little thought or question, in the distance I can faintly hear: "if it's new, its gotta' be good; so I gotta' have it - now!"

Fine (well, almost)

XXIV

The closing story of one man's mission

THE LITERACY MOVEMENT--WHAT DOES BRAILLE MUSIC HAVE TO DO WITH IT?

by Richard Taesch (1993)

Within the science of education, there is much to be learned from the special problems confronted by the blind student. As educators, whether music, academic, or the combination of both, we share a common responsibility for developing and maintaining usable communication medias for our students. As professional music teachers, few of us would question the value of the music reading skill as an indispensable and tangible communication medium.

Unfortunately, not all students are given the opportunity of access to the musical medium we know as print or braille. Some music teachers might be surprised to find that many students, sighted or blind, are not taught to read music at all. In pop music situations, often reading is considered cumbersome and unnecessary. As with the printed word, music reading is an issue of literacy. No person should be denied personal access to information and the freedom of choice it provides.

Why then is there so much illiteracy? Is there a correlation between academic and music illiteracy? Who has failed to show the earliest learner that literary and music reading is important and within reach? Who has told the blind learner that braille music reading is only a luxury, and that he or she must remain dependent upon recordings made by the sighted? Perhaps the answers to some of these questions can be found in attitudes and indifference within our own ranks. There does, indeed, seem to be a definite correlation with respect to resistance in all types of literacy.

What Is Wrong With This Picture?

Inspiration for this article came at a much unexpected moment. While attending a meeting of certified braille transcribers, I was exposed to the news that the Braille Literacy Bill, SB. 701, had been dropped due to lack of support and interest. The bill was to provide access in all schools to braille learning for blind students. That very afternoon while speaking with a coordinator of music programs for the blind, I was told that this department did not encourage braille music reading. I was told in so many words that music reading for the blind was impractical, too slow, and generally not preferred by their blind performers. It was much easier to learn from recordings made for them, and that it was impractical to memorize everything. This information, incidentally, was being provided by a sighted person in charge of this program. When I asked if the person knew braille music or anything about it, the answer was expectedly, "no!"

As a music teacher developing a new program for braille music, I was deeply wounded. "Have I spent all these years envisioning an idea only to discover little support from blind students or those in charge of educating them?"

As the wheels in my mind continued to churn, my disappointment turned to anger, then to a strong sense of responsibility. One of my questions about illiteracy had been answered! The blame cannot be placed upon the innocent learner who has not been informed properly nor given the choice to become independent and "literate."

There is a study called "The Leipzig Connection" (Paolo Lionni, Heron Books 1993). It traces the birth of experimental psychology and its effect on education today. The study follows the downgrading of education based upon a concept that children are taught to conform and only to serve the needs of an orderly society. We are not to become creative individuals capable of making our own choices. This concept does not consider teachers instructors, but "designers of learning experiences." If this is true even only in theory, then we have much to be concerned about - and some profound possibilities regarding some difficult questions.

As music teachers we know, perhaps better than any educator, the value of teaching independence, creativity, and the right to be individual. Who better is in a position to help turn the tide, and to begin with literacy in our own music studios?

Solfege - Hands-on Vs. Hands-off

The European concept of solfege or music reading being taught before an instrument is played is as old as music itself. Teachers often find that Asian students who have been taught in this way are musically superior to American born children. Why is this? As a teacher of the guitar for thirty-three [62 in 2023] years, I have experienced a phenomenon that, during an oral instructional session, if the fingers touch the strings, the brain seems to leave the body. The mind closes off, drooling begins, and the avenues of communication are severely restricted. Why is this?

With the "hands-off" approach, the instrument is viewed as an inanimate object. It is only capable of reproducing what the performer emotionally, intellectually, and technically is capable of. In America, the instrument is the primary focus. It is the "toy"-- the material object that captures the interest. It has a soul, a personality, and in some cases, has even synthesized the musician.

Though it is true that music is first perceived by the ear, if the next focal point is the toy, the tangible intellectual force behind the art is then by-passed. The hands-off approach, on the other hand, allows the musical mind to develop more quickly and freely, unbiased by another interpretation as first exposure. Tools of interpretation are then applied through prudent training and pedagogy. The "tangible communication medium" of music is now set in place.

By Ear-Alone Vs. By Music

Perhaps more in the area of braille music is the argument of learning by ear vs. learning to read music. When playing by ear, stimuli enter via the ear senses. With the sight or touch medium (as is braille reading), the intellect must first decipher the tangible communication medium. The ear and the eye methods - much to the surprise of ear-only supporters - have everything in common. Both reach to an outside source to receive and process data. The ideal, of course, is to merge both senses in order to "hear with the eye (or touch)," and to "see with the ear." In this way, the blind and sighted learner or performer share the same means of input.

To learn solely by using the finished product (pre-recorded music) as a model, denies students access to their own unique interpretive process. There must be a vehicle separate from the finished product. The medium itself must be flexible and capable of varied application. Using the finished product for a pattern as in the ear-only approach, cannot replace such a medium.

To learn by listening only is merely a form of plagiarism. Reproduction is strongly influenced by the interpretation of the version being copied. For blind performer, there is little opportunity for personal interpretation of data initially perceived through aural communication. Even with "talking books" for the blind, the language/communication medium is being interpreted and translated by the intellect. Pictures and meanings are then formed and evaluated, accepted or questioned. Therefore, music by ear alone is dependency upon performance by the sighted--there is no translation process taking place.

The right to choose the translation process should be available to all. For the blind learner, it seems the choice not to read is based upon a lack of exposure to the braille music medium at the earliest levels. From what source does this prejudice come? Surely it cannot come from an experienced teacher of music who is, at least, aware of the logical clarity of the braille music language intended by Louis Braille himself! A music teacher in charge of a blind student need not know anything about braille to recognize the right of that student to make a choice for music literacy. Louis Braille, by the way, was a blind piano teacher!

A Case for Music Literacy

Not all music teachers will have the opportunity to teach a blind student during their careers. Some teachers prefer not to teach blind students. All teachers, however, can benefit from a better understanding of any communication problems encountered in the teaching profession. Allow me to share a few pros and cons I have encountered in the case for music reading by the blind:

Argument: "The blind learner is still dependent upon the sighted transcriber for braille music, so what is the difference?"
Answer: So is the sighted learner dependent upon the creation of the printed page for resource music aside from previously recorded music. With written music, print or braille, the playing field becomes equal for blind or sighted learners.
Argument: "There are too many symbols!"
Answer: Not really. In print a note appears on a staff position; in braille a note has an octave mark placed in front of it. Often a group of notes will not require octave marks; in print all notes require a staff position. In print, notes are blackened or open to indicate values, etc. In braille, a simple dot position in the note cell indicates value.
Argument: "The sighted performer can scan the music visually for live performance. There is less need for memorization; braille music is much too cumbersome to be used by a blind performer."

Answer: Once again, such a statement is an obvious case of the sighted thinking and choosing for the blind. Instant sight reading is totally irrelevant to the value of the "tangible communication medium."

Whether braille or print, the communication medium of music is still a new language that must be developed early in the process. The initial speed of interpretation is again irrelevant, and should not be a deciding factor against the case for music or braille music literacy!

Braille Music and the Educator

Written music is extremely important in educational situations. Consider the blind student in the study of composition at the college level. Would anyone recommend the study of orchestration and arranging without being able to see the range and movement of the various instruments? Who is going to record a three-hundred-page theory or harmony text with music examples on audio? Does this mean the blind student is excluded from music courses? The blind student will be excluded from many things if totally dependent upon the sighted.

Other examples include lyric and chord symbol placement for basic accompaniment. Jazz music lead sheets, chord progressions, improvisation layouts, and song form are not easily approached by ear only. The ear is the final judge, however, not always the best way to demonstrate musical logic and architectural form.

Braille Music Basics for the Layperson

It is not the purpose of this study to convince music teachers that they should undertake the study of braille music. On the contrary, the intention is to provide a view of this side of your profession. Whether you will admit it or not, the cause for literacy affects us all. Music is manifested in sound. As teachers, how better our depth of understanding can become if we possess a view of those who hear in darkness.

The braille cell is a six-dot configuration. Each cell can represent a letter, a number, a whole word, or a musical note depending on context and accompanying signs. Although music braille is separate from the Literary Code, there is a "facsimile" form used for simple lead sheet music that does not require knowledge of the Music Code. Such a format can even be used by teachers who do not know braille at all. This format is used for beginning students where words and the placement of chord symbols are desirable.

In braille music, the braille literary letter "D" is used as the solfege symbol, "Do." This braille note is "C," and the remaining music alphabet follows consecutively, re, mi, fa, etc. This is a "fixed-Do" system with C always remaining as *Do*. For braille "touch-singing," numbers are initially assigned to the scale steps just as in print solfege. The number 1 is assigned to the first scale step thereby creating a "movable-Do" system.

There are two [side-by side] columns of dots numbered vertically 1-2-3, and 4-5-6. The bottom of the cell, dots 3 and 6, are used to indicate values. Dots 4, 5, and 6 are used before a note cell to indicate octave positions such as first octave, second octave, etc. Solfege symbols can then be applied for either movable or a fixed Do system.

For piano students, one hand touches the braille while the other plays the music. After both hands have been played, the student assembles a section to be memorized. For string instruments, one hand can hypothetically play all of the music by feel first. For the vocalist, singing can take place immediately while touch-reading the braille music.

Conclusion

Throughout my career I have experienced growth in the field of music teaching even while learning skills not directly related to music. Hopefully, this study can provide a new aspect of the music reading skill for teachers. If the decision not to support music reading, whether braille or print, is made by those who know little about it, then what hope do we have? Knowledge and information must be shared, and willingness to consider all forms of communication must remain open. If those known to be experts in the field of braille music - many of them blind - are also successful teachers of music, then I invite you to draw your own conclusions. We must provide our students with every available means of self-reliance. Give them the means to function as self-reliant individuals, and watch them grow more quickly and their willingness to contribute to our world increase.

I would like to conclude with the following quotation by the Rev. R. Inman:

> " *The great teacher never strives to explain his vision--he simply invites you to stand beside him and see for yourself.* "

* * *

A final tribute

To Dr. Burgess, all of the lonely crusaders, and to all of the givers:
We did the work
And I trust that the rest will take care of itself - R.T.

The Beginning - Opus 2

> " I have hiked hundreds and hundreds of miles with nary the need to be any particular places other than where I have been - R. Taesch "

A facsimile letter (text only) of appreciation dated 4/10/2006

10 April 2006
Dear Richard,
At long last, we bring you Louis! Thanks so much for your wonderful, informative assistance with the music section.

A *Touch of Genius* brings together for the first time:

- 31 extant letters, some written by Louis's own hand
- 118 never-before-published documents, photographs, and engravings
- factual biography drawn from primary sources

My best,
D... C...
v-p/publishing

*Louis Braille - A Touch of Genius
by C. Michael Mellor-
Published by National Braille Press - NBP - www.braille.com

ABOUT THE AUTHOR

Richard Taesch was founder and retired chair of Braille Music Division at Southern California Conservatory of Music - Est. 1971-2013. He founded *Music Education Network for The Visually Impaired -* MENVI in 1997, and authored *An Introduction to Music for the Blind Student* series, *A Blind Music Student's College Survival Guide*, and textbooks for the guitar while serving as Guitar Department chair for the SCCM since 1976. A music educator since 1961, he has been listed in "Who's Who in America" since 2003, and recognized as Recipient for the Albert Nelson Marquis Lifetime Achievement Award in 2017.

ACKNOWLEDGMENTS

My deepest and heartfelt appreciation goes to Mr. Gabriel Chavarria - Production Manager for Infinity/Fast Pencil/Opyrus Publishing. His patience, dedication, superb expertise, and sensitivity to my special needs, has been the primary catalyst that has brought this remembrance - Winter through Autumn - to reality.

In an unfinished season such as autumn here, acknowledgments seem to be few, as the story is still a work in progress. As such, I have chosen to list the precious few that follow - those who gave so much encouragement to me, having read and / or publicly reviewed *For all too soon*. Reviews for *Summer's Memory* will appear later in a second edition of *For all too soon*.

First and foremost, I wish to thank Ms. Christine Jelloian - a former student, and graduate of the Southern California Conservatory of Music (SCCM) composition department. Ms. Jelloian later served bravely on the troubled SCCM board, and partnered with her older brother to organize a very grandiose and catered fundraiser. The event never reached its goal, as promises made by some who pledged were never realized.

Just as the first chapter of *Summer's Memory* was beginning, Richard was still not quite sure where or how to begin. Christine had been keeping me informed of a special competitive amateur musician event that she had been following; she expressed her thoughts regarding a favored blind-autistic performer. My advocacy background and protective instincts, tended to raise some hair on my proverbial back regarding

ACKNOWLEDGMENTS

patronizing by some promoters; thus the direction of Chapter One was born.

Others, either by email response or formal website reviews, are as follows: Robb Navrides - Senior Supervising Sound Editor, Formosa Group, Hollywood, CA.(television post production); Dr. James Aldrich - Retired Statistics and Research Methods Professor, California State University, Northridge - CSUN, author of *White House Hobo,* © *2021;* Pearle Lun, a former student from ca. age 9, graduate of Stanford University; Mrs. Adeline Lopez, daughter of Crescent Valley Mobile Home Park manager, Angie Leano (see *The Great Quake of 1994 -* "For all too soon"), great grandmother, and my dear neighbor here on *34th Street;* Mr. Roger Biasi - retired professor of auto shop, [currently known as] Los Angeles Trade Technical College. Roger indicated to Dr. Aldrich that he enjoyed getting to know Richard through reading *For all too soon;* Valerie Gaer-Sandler holds a very special place in Richard's voyage. Affectionately named "Noah" for fun in *For all too soon,* Valerie braved the best and the worst as Director of Development for the SCCM at its troubled La Canada campus. A graduate of New England Conservatory of Music masters program, her patience and musical creativity is a stunning example for all.

My sincere thanks to my friend, Dr. James P. Kraft - Professor, Department of History University of Hawaiʻi at Manoa. *Jim* offered extremely valuable suggestions for Chapter 11, *Careers,* which includes my contribution for an episode in his first book - "**Stage to Studio**" (referenced and linked in that chapter).

A very special - although belated - thank you goes to my friend and neighbor, Noboru Kosora - retired professional chemist. In casual conversation, Noboru inspired the addition of the highly applicable term,"... or nothing at all" in Chapter 28 of *For all too soon.*

And most significantly, the last has been intentionally reserved for Victoria Seaborn. Ms. Seaborn is a preschool educator, past director, and professional consultant who was the first to post a public review about *For all too soon.* Victoria made no hesitation to express recognition of the meaning for: *Just do the work*. "Summer's Memory" is dedicated to her, and to a little dog that she loved named, *Kindness* (See Introduction).

Clearly, there are many other folks and inspirations for an amateur writer to help write his or her own remembrance. Those I've recognized here are just a few that hold a special place in this autumn season of my years.

Cover photo: Pacific Crest Trail at dusk, looking west towards Windy Gap - Angeles National Forest, California

Cover design & photo by Richard Taesch

www.ingramcontent.com/pod-product-compliance
Lightning Source LLC
Chambersburg PA
CBHW071200070526
44584CB00019B/2860